WITHDRAWN

LAMBEAU LEGENDS
PACKER PROFILES OF COURAGE ★

by David Zimmerman

BOOKS

Published by Eagle Books
P.O Box 253
Hales Corners, WI 53130
414-525-1601

Copyright © 2008 by David Zimmerman
All rights reserved, including the right of
reproduction in whole or part.

Jacket designed by Lindsay Peters
Printed by Sengraph Communications, Inc.

United States of America

ISBN 13:978-1-882987-15-3

Acknowledgements

Thanks to my wife, Peg, who encouraged me to get on with writing this Packers book I had been talking about for such a long time.

Thanks to Bob Harlan, Packers chairman emeritus for his encouragement in the project.

Thanks to Tom Murphy, director and archivist of the Packers Hall of Fame for his help in obtaining photo and background information.

I'm grateful for the hard work and time my son, Joe, and his wife, Kim, put into typing the original manuscript.

Tip of the hat to Lindsay Peters for his unique cover design.

Finally, thanks to journalist David Claerbaut for his excellent profile on Vince Lombardi.

*To Lynn Dickey, the epitome of the courage
it takes to play in the NFL,
and to the many who sacrificed
so much physically to play
for the Green Bay Packers.*

PACKER PROFILES OF COURAGE

Contents

Foreword
   By Bob Harlan, Green Bay Packers Chairman Emeritus i

Preface iii

Earl 'Curley' Lambeau 1
   Bulldog-like courage to keep Green Bay in the the NFL

Vince Lombardi 15
   The courage of his convictions

Arnie Herber 25
   Hometown hero overcomes ridicule to become a star

Clark Hinkle 35
   Brute force was his game

Tony Canadeo 43
   A hero for all seasons

Bob Mann 63
   The first African-American to play for the Packers.
   It took a unique courage to break the 'color barrier'

Tobin Rote 69
   When courage didn't result in team success

Bart Starr 77
   Perseverance in overcoming prolonged adversity

Jerry Kramer 93
   Uncommon comeback from life-threatening accidents,
   nothing short of miraculous

Ray Nitschke 101
   The courage to overcome self-destruction
   to become the best linebacker in Packer history

Fred 'Fuzzy' Thurston 111
   Conquering adversity off the field –
   an inspirational story.

PACKER PROFILES OF COURAGE

Willie Wood 121
    Overcoming extreme odds as a Packer walk-on
    to make it all the way to the Pro Football Hall of Fame

The 1962 Season 129
    Team Courage on Display: The Packers' 1962 Season
    chosen as a prime example of 'team courage.'

Ken Bowman and Larry McCarren 147
    In the center of pain

The 'Ice Bowl' 153
    Packers' 1967 championship game against Cowboys,
    in bitter cold, test of wills and display of courage

Lynn Dickey 163
    An amazing display of grit
    in overcoming crippling injuries

LeRoy Butler 173
    An inspiring story of overcoming
    disability and poverty

Donald Driver 179
    Provides hope in overcoming financial hardships
    with lessons learned as a youth

Brett Favre 138
    An amazing career that displayed
    a special kind of courage

Postscript 195

About the Author 196

Foreword

In the long, glorious history of the Green Bay Packers, many men have displayed a wide variety of unusual courage and inner strength. As fate would have it, these characteristics were manifested not only in the field of play, but also in their ordinary lives.

All those who have played or coached for the Packers are exceptional athletes with extraordinary talents, but they are still subject to life's wide range of experiences, just like the rest of us.

The game of football is much like the game of life, where fortunes often take unexpected twists, sometimes leading to success, other times to tragedy or misfortune.

How individuals cope with all that life renders, defines their true character. The description of the men on the following pages are graphic examples of that premise.

— Bob Harlan
Green Bay Packers Chairman Emeritus

Preface

During World War I, but before the United States officially entered the war, a few brave men became America's first fighter pilots. They joined the legendary Lafayette Escadrille, that flimsy, open-cockpit biplane, for the French against the Germans.

Defying almost impossible odds – the pilot death rate was nearly 75 percent – these courageous young men distinguished themselves in a manner that none before had dared. They became true heroes who experienced triumph, and loss in the chaos of World War I.

In classic display of bravado, the French captain shouted to each American pilot as he climbed into his airplane for his next mission, **"Courage!"** And it took raw courage for these young men, to utterly risk their lives for what they considered a worthy cause.

We have tried to capture some of that same kind of extreme courage, displayed in many ways, by different men, in different times, on and off the football field – true heroes nevertheless – who also experienced triumph, tragedy and loss in their own lives.

— David Zimmerman
Director, Green Bay Packers Hall of Fame

Rare Courage

Football is physically demanding at any level – from high school through college. To play in the NFL – take it up several notches. The players are bigger, faster, and stronger.

Action at the pro level can be turbulent and violent. Too often, it becomes bone-crunching rough. Bodies take a constant beating. Many a gifted athlete has experienced a promising career in the pros get cut short with a crippling injury.

Lambeau Legends – Packer Profiles of Courage captures a unique courage displayed in many ways by different men in different times on and off the football field. True Packer heroes that experienced triumph, tragedy, and loss in their own lives.

There are 18 Packers profiled in the chapters that follow and of those 18, there are eight of them in the prestigious Pro Football Hall of Fame in Canton, Ohio. All except two were also honored to be inducted into the Packer Hall of Fame. While they all have been recognized for their success on the field, I attempted to show an additional quality each possessed – a rare kind of courage – both on and off the football field.

Even though these men were gifted athletes or coaches who became some of the best in the profession, they gave evidence to the fact they also are not exempt from life's ups and downs. Their real-life stories give evidence to their character.

Earl 'Curley' Lambeau
*Bulldog-like courage to keep
Green Bay in the NFL*

Courage in life is measured in many ways. In Earl 'Curley' Lambeau's case, courage was displayed in the bulldog-like actions he took to keep Green Bay a part of the NFL, in spite of almost impossible odds. His exceptional efforts didn't just span a short burst of time, but endured over a long, laborious 30-year stretch.

Oftentimes during that period, any one of several circumstances would have been enough to be the death song for the Green Bay Packers had it not been for Lambeau's tenacity.

As successful, profitable, well-established a club, and as entrenched in the NFL as the Packers are today, it is undoubtedly difficult for anyone to comprehend how they could have been so precariously close to disappearing from the pro football scene, like so many other teams did through those early years of the league.

It was primarily through the single-minded determination of Lambeau that the Packers survived those uncertain early years of the team. He was their coach, their leader, their inspiration, and their organizer. He even personally picked the players. But most important, he was a winner. He won more games than any other NFL coach during his

30-plus years. Had he been a loser, the Packers would have been gone long ago.

Earl 'Curly' Lambeau was truly one-of-a-kind. He was an individual who comes around only once in a great while to make a profound difference, the kind who makes an impact, and leaves an imprint for generations to come.

As a youth, Lambeau played football with such passion and devotion that it eventually parlayed him and his hometown of Green Bay, Wisconsin, into the national spotlight. With Lambeau's unbridled enthusiasm and wholehearted dedication to his football team, both those who played the game and the citizens of the city formed a bond so uncommon that it has also been called one-of-a-kind.

The smaller city of Green Bay competing against teams from much larger cities created the compelling 'David vs. Goliath' story again and again through these many years. The tenacity that Lambeau exuded rallied the Packers in their early years in the NFL and supported them in other trying seasons. It made possible the Packers' advance from the scrubby turf of an open field in 1919 to the best-known outdoor sports stadium in the nation – Lambeau Field.

The stadium where the Packers play today is named after the man who organized the team at age 21 and led it as captain and coach for the first 31 years of its existence. Starting the team as a city club for two years, 1919 to 1920, he took the Packers into what would, in 1921, become the National Football League.

Lambeau was a solid player from 1919 until he retired from playing after the 1928 season. As head coach from 1919 through 1949, he compiled an amazing record. His Packer teams won six National Football League titles – three in a row from 1929 through 1931, then again in 1936, 1939 and 1944. He compiled a 31-year record of 248-108-23, for a fantastic .685 winning percentage. Piling up 209 wins from 1921-49, Lambeau had more victories in that period than any other NFL coach.

Lambeau coached in the NFL for 33 years, including 29 with the Packers. Only George Halas coached longer. His

PROFILES OF COURAGE • CURLY LAMBEAU

In his senior year, Lambeau's high school yearbook reflected his captivating personality.

Lambeau was a star for Green Bay East High School where he lettered in football four years.

Lambeau (center) also excelled at track in high school.

As captain and coach of his high school team, Lambeau (far right with football) would lead his team to an undefeated season his senior year.

NFL record of 226-132-22 trails only Don Shula and Tom Landry, and his six NFL championships are second to none.

In the nine-year stretch between 1936 and 1944, Lambeau's Packers won 75 percent of all their regular NFL season games, won the Western Division Championship four times, placed second for five seasons, and captured three World Championships. The Packers' record during this remarkable time span was 73-21-4. No other NFL coach came close to matching Lambeau's success during this period.

After each of the six World Championships, Green Bay citizens treated Lambeau like a conquering hero, their knight in shining armor. He was the city's favorite son, the hometown boy who made good. On cold December nights, tens of thousands would greet the team for exuberant title celebrations. Parades and all-night parties would cap off each triumph. It was an unbelievable time of adulation and jubilation.

Lambeau became a national celebrity throughout the 1930's and 1940's. His accomplishments, charming personality, and the 'David vs. Goliath' theme caught the fancy of journalists in all the major newspapers and magazines of the time. The *Saturday Evening Post, Look, Life* and numerous other national publications carried feature stories on Lambeau, and he was interviewed hundreds of times, as the small-town Green Bay and its Packers became the darlings of the nation.

Lambeau was inducted into the Pro Football Hall of Fame in 1963, its first year in existence, and was later inducted into the Packer Hall of Fame (1970) and the Wisconsin Hall of Fame. The contributions he made to the game of football, the NFL, the city of Green Bay, and the state of Wisconsin were major. He gave the team and the city of Green Bay unequaled national prominence between 1921 and 1949.

Lambeau was the Green Bay Packers during the first 31 years of their existence. It was his team representing his town. He started it, picked the players, provided the drive

PROFILES OF COURAGE • CURLY LAMBEAU

Lambeau (top row, third from left) played one season (1918) at Notre Dame for legendary coach Knute Rockne. The famed George Gipp (fourth from left, top row) was his teammate.
Notre Dame Archives

Curly and Marguerite, high school sweethearts, were married in 1919, the first year the Packers were formed.
Tom Murphy, private collection photo

The first Packer team, 1919. They outscored their opponents 565 to 12 and won 10, lost 1. Lambeau, coach and captain, is holding the ball, center, just behind the first row. George Calhoun, team manager is far right, back row.
Packer Hall of Fame photo

and motivation, and ran it with an iron hand until near the end of his tenure with the Packers in 1949. He alone found the players he wanted, negotiated their contacts, handled team travel, and even designed team uniforms.

No one close to the Packer organization questions the fact that without Lambeau, there would be no Green Bay Packers today. That is some legacy!

In his early years, Lambeau was an energetic, gifted athlete with a charming personality that captured the hearts of his teachers and classmates alike. Blessed with good looks and a strong body, Lambeau stood out among his peers. He was bright and extremely extroverted. As he assembled his successful Packer teams in the 1920's, he demonstrated his natural leadership skills along with a knack for selling. He successfully sold his hometown, his players and his fans on his Packers throughout the beginning stages of the fledgling team.

After his first World Championship in 1929, and through the glory years of six World Championships up into the mid-1940's, his personality and character would undergo gradual changes. As the team grew more successful and his image developed into a larger-than-life character, his passion for winning grew even stronger. He became more intense, impatient, and impulsive.

At the same time, Lambeau became more creative, disciplined, and focused than at any time in his life. Winning became an obsession. Continued success also inflated his ego, which in turn, had a tendency to give him a distorted view of his own importance.

Lambeau's relationship with the press, for the most part, was cordial. His coverage by newspaper sportswriters between 1930 and 1955 was extensive, not only in Green Bay and Milwaukee, but also around the nation. Art Daley of the Green Bay *Press-Gazette*, who covered the Packers in the 1940's, respected and feared Lambeau at the same time. He could never get very close to him.

Lee Remmel, who also covered the Packers for the *Press-Gazette* in the 1940's and is now retired executive director of

PROFILES OF COURAGE • CURLY LAMBEAU

Lambeau plots out strategy in a pre-game meeting in a New York hotel, preparing for the NFL championship game in December 1936 against the Giants. Front row includes Charles "Buckets" Goldenberg (left) and Don Hutson (far right).

UPI-Bettman

public relations of the Packers, called Lambeau an, "...imaginative, impatient visionary with vast energy, who had an indomitable will to win."

Sportswriter Lloyd Larson of the *Milwaukee Sentinel* once said, "Lambeau has a great knack of spotting potential stars and selling them on coming to Green Bay."

Bud Lea, long-time sportswriter for the *Milwaukee Sentinel* said, "It was Lambeau's persistence that kept the Packers alive."

Reflections on Lambeau came from many other reporters, too. Arthur Daley, well known sportswriter for the *New York Times*, wrote, "Curly Lambeau was the Packers."

Arch Ward, sports editor of the *Chicago Tribune* and long-time acquaintance of Lambeau, one said, "My association with Lambeau, which spans more than two decades, has been one of unbroken pleasantness."

Oliver Kuechle, one-time sports editor for the *Milwaukee Journal* who covered the Packers during most of Lambeau's tenure at Green Bay, once wrote, "Lambeau dominated his teams, bent them to his will. He was a genius in the way he inspired and led his teams." He added, at the time of Lambeau's death, a statement that carries a great truth, "Few men anywhere have ever done as much for their hometown as Lambeau for his."

Anyone familiar with the Packers knows the legendary story of how Lambeau was encouraged by Green Bay newspaper sports editor, George Calhoun, to start a city team in the summer of 1919. Legend has it, Lambeau went to his boss, Frank Peck, of Indian Packing (later Acme Packing Co.) and asked if the company would sponsor a city team and help buy football uniforms, equipment and balls. Peck responded with $500 and the use of a company-owned, vacant field the next to his plant, where Lambeau's team could hold practice. At the second meeting of the interested players, Lambeau was elected captain of the new team.

The 21-year-old Lambeau did such a good job of rounding up some of the best players in the state, that the team crushed every team they played. Curly scheduled games with teams from Marinette, Menominee, New London, Ishpeming, and Stambaugh, all in the Upper Peninsula of Michigan. He also got Racine and Sheboygan to agree to games. Altogether, he secured eleven playing dates. The team outscored its opponents over the entire season by a staggering 565 points to 12.

The following year, 1920, was just as successful, with Lambeau's team outscoring the teams it played, 227 to 24. In 1921, Calhoun and Lambeau heard of a new pro football league called the American Professional Football Association being formed. The league name was changed a few years later to the National Football League. Calhoun and Lambeau put up $100 and they were now in the 'big leagues.'

The Packers were about to become a team in a legitimate professional football league. The Lambeau name was destined to become permanently etched in the annals of the game.

While there would be 21 teams in the league that year, some would not even make it to the end of the season before going broke. In fact, there would be 49 different teams competing in the pro football league at one time or another during the Roaring Twenties. Small- and mid-sized towns like Frankford, Akron, Canton, Rock Island, Dayton, Pottsville, Hammond, Columbus, Muncie, Louisville, Racine, Toledo, and Duluth made up the league before larger cities such as Chicago, Cleveland, Milwaukee, New York, Minneapolis, and Detroit joined during the 1920's.

Under Lambeau's leadership, the Packers were one of the most successful teams of the new pro football league through the 1920's and 1930's. However, it wasn't all 'peaches and cream' for the Packers in the 1920's and 1930's. They almost ran out of money a few times; Lambeau and the city leaders held fund-raising events and pulled the team out of serious financial problems. Once the team was sued when a fan fell out of the stands in old City Stadium. The Packers had to file bankruptcy to get enough time to raise the cash to pay off the settlement and keep the team alive.

Their winning record and unmatched success by the other NFL teams in the 1920's and 1930's were really the major reasons why the Packers were able to get off their backs financially so often and remain in the NFL. The fans of Wisconsin loved their team and did whatever it took to keep it alive.

Another close call came in 1949, when the Packers almost went broke again. Once again, the fans of Wisconsin helped raise enough money to keep the team alive.

On October 29, about a third of the way through the 1929 season, the stock market crashed, ending a post-World War I period of prosperity that has been dubbed the Jazz Age and the Golden Age of Sports. The crash brought on the Great Depression.

Like most other enterprises, professional football also suffered. At the end of the 1929 season, with the Depression's effect barely perceptible, the Pottsville Maroons, New York Yankees, Detroit Wolverines, and Duluth Eskimos all called it quits. In 1930, the Boston Bulldogs, Buffalo Bisons, and Dayton Triangle disbanded. The 1931 casualties were the Minneapolis Red Jackets and the Newark Tornadoes. In 1932, the Providence Steam Rollers, the first-year Cleveland Indians, and the Frankford Yellow Jackets folded. The Yellow Jackets didn't even last to the end of the season. By 1932, in the depth of the Depression, NFL membership fell to eight teams, the smallest in its history. By then, Green Bay would be the only small-city team left standing in the NFL.

But through it all, the Packers not only survived, but they also excelled, winning NFL championships in 1929, 1930, and 1931. They added two more championships, in 1939 and 1949, before the decline began.

After winning the NFL championship in 1944, Lambeau slipped from being the honored, revered coach. Over the next five years, several key factors led to Lambeau's fall. The descent began gradually. By 1949, he was in his first free-fall.

A new pro football league, the All-American Football Conference (AAFC), began in 1946, and with backing from extremely wealthy owners, took many of the more-talented college players. Many of Lambeau's college draft picks from 1946 through 1949 were less than mediocre because too many of the athletes whom Green Bay wanted went to higher paying AAFC teams. The Packer talent would become inferior to other NFL teams.

From 1947 through 1949, Lambeau also was at odds with the Packers' board of directors. The fact that the team was losing also hurt. Furthermore, with City Stadium capable of holding only 25,000 fans, the Packers could not draw the same kinds of crowds as other NFL teams in Chicago, Detroit, Los Angeles, Philadelphia, New York, and Washington, D.C., could The Packers began to see their profits slip away, to the point that, midway through the 1949 season, the club was on the verge of bankruptcy.

With all of the negative circumstances coming into play, the Packers began to lose at an unparalleled pace from 1946 through 1949. The result was an ignominious end to an extraordinary 31-year relationship between Earl Lambeau and the Green Bay Packers.

Lambeau's resignation was announced on January 30, 1950. The words, "Curly quit the Packers!" swept through Green Bay on the first day of February. People ignored the sub-zero weather and gathered in cliques on street corners, at luncheon tables, and in cocktail lounges around town to discuss Lambeau's resignation. The *Press-Gazette* had Lambeau's resignation splashed across the front page. The *Chicago Tribune* featured the story on their sports page.

Most people were little interested in the fact that Lambeau had accepted the head coaching position and vice-presidency of the Chicago Cardinals. Instead, they focused the discussion on the fact that he had left the Packers, whom he had helped bring into being 31 years prior and had developed into a professional football power.

Oliver Kuechle, sports editor for the *Milwaukee Journal* and close to the Packer situation for over 20 years during Lambeau's tenure, wrote a summary some time later:

"Whatever the basis for the difference, however, personal

PROFILES OF COURAGE • CURLY LAMBEAU

Lambeau at the height of his coaching career with the Packers in the late 1930s and early 1940s.

Lambeau with Ted Fritsch in the locker room after the Packers victory in the NFL Championship. It would be Lambeau's last championship. After 1944 the team began to decline.
Packer Hall of Fame photo

Packers celebrate in dressing room after game. Players lift up Coach Curly Lambeau and Ted Fritsch (#64) after winning their 6th NFL Championship in 1944.
Tom Pigeon Private Collection photo

PROFILES OF COURAGE • CURLY LAMBEAU

Lambeau's handsome appearance coupled with his outgoing personality made him an appealing interview for newspapers and magazines. In 1946, Lambeau convinced the Packer board to purchase Rockwood Lodge *(shown here)*, 14 miles northeast of Green Bay for player housing and training facility.
Packer Hall of Fame photo

or otherwise, the sum total was the same. Here was one of the greatest little organizations in football, Lambeau's organization, no longer fighting jealously against the big city rival on the field, and fighting successfully, but fighting bitterly within itself. Something had to give. So Lambeau resigned and the era ended. He was the Packers. The adventure of a small town football team in the big league came to an end. The world champion Packers who made Green Bay a household word."

Indeed, Lambeau was gone, closing the final chapter on 31 years as a Packer and assembling the most wins of any pro football coach up until that time. In those 31 years, the Packers had only three losing seasons. No Packer coach will ever match, or even come close to, the long-term success of Lambeau. Only George Halas surpassed this NFL winning percentage during this time, and his winning record was only one percentage point better than Lambeau's.

Six championship flags hung limp at old City Stadium on the bitterly cold day in February. They were reminders of a distant past – of far better times. Thousands standing and cheering in the cold December nights at the train depot to welcome home their champion Packers in 1929, 1930, 1931, 1936, 1939, and 1944 were but a faded dream.

The car horns, train and factory whistles, fire engine sirens, and church bells that had blasted and rung out, celebrating the David vs. Goliath victories, were now silent. The Packer victory banquets, all-night partying and dancing were now just memories. There would be no more celebrating Packer champions – until a new hero would arrive ten years later.

Vince Lombardi
The courage of his convictions

If Lambeau founded and developed the Packers, Vince Lombardi rescued the franchise from oblivion.

When Lombardi became head coach and general manager in 1959, he made it very clear he would be in complete charge of the once proud and glorious NFL franchise which was now in a disordered mess. The Packers had gone eleven seasons without winning more games than they lost. The Packers' record from 1948 thru the 1958 season was 37-93-2, a lousy winning percentage of .288.

Lombardi came on strong. He told the 45-member Packers board of directors he would exercise completely the courage of his convictions, and would be in complete control. One member was to have said, "Who the hell does he think he is?" to which the other was to have answered, "He is the savior of the Green Bay Packers."

Lombardi went from savior to legend in his nine years with the Packers. He won five NFL crowns in nine years. Add in his conference championship in 1960, after which the Pack fell to the Eagles in Philadelphia, and you have six championship years.

When you consider that his 1963 squad did not win a title but registered an 11-2-1 mark, you can see that, with a break here or there (he had lost Starr for a good portion of

1963), he may well have had seven championships in nine seasons. That would leave just two less-than-championship-level years – 1959 and 1964.

Ironically, however, the 1959 season was arguably Lombardi's greatest accomplishment. He took over a team that had not had a winning season in a dozen years. In the season immediately preceding Lombardi's arrival, the squad had bottomed out with a 1-10-1 mark, putting the very existence of the franchise in jeopardy.

In the legendary mentor's first year, however, the team catapulted to a 7-5 mark, a pick-up of 5-1/2 games in a twelve-game season. No previous Packer squad had won seven games since 1944.

That is how Vince Lombardi did it in 1959 – Determination, Discipline, and Defense.

In the years to follow, determination never wavered, discipline remained a cornerstone, and both the offense and defense posted league-leading numbers. Those were great years.

Green Bay became 'Titletown,' the 'Ice Bowl' became part of football lore, Lombardi became the coaching icon, and the Packers became the yardstick against which future champions in every sport have been measured.

He was no president nor senator, no journalist, nor social critic, no evangelist, nor philosopher. He was a football coach who died long ago, in the late summer of 1970.

Today, however, Vincent Thomas Lombardi is more than merely alive. He is everywhere. Leaders are said to be 'Lombardi-like.' Lombardi-isms such as 'mental toughness,' 'pursuit of excellence,' and 'second effort,' are part of our daily lexicon.

He continues to be quoted, books are still written about him, and those whose lives he touched state that hardly a day goes by that they do not think about him. In brief, Vince Lombardi is still relevant, still dominant, still a driving force in the new millennium, long after other great political figures, popular religious leaders, revered news commentators, and yes, lionized football coaches have been forgotten.

PROFILES OF COURAGE • VINCE LOMBARDI

Mr. and Mrs. Vincent T. Lombardi arrived in Green Bay on a cold February day in 1959 where Vince was to take over as head coach and general manager of the Green Bay Packers. Thus began the Lombardi Era in Packer history.
Lefebvre photo

When Lombardi took over the Packers in 1959, he told the board he would exercise the courage of his convictions and would be in complete control.
Packer Hall of Fame photo

Lombardi used determination, discipline and defense to begin turning the Packers into winners.
Packer Hall of Fame photo

Green Bay became Titletown, the Ice Bowl became part of football lore and Lombardi became the coaching icon.
Packer Hall of Fame photo

Why? In large part it is because he was bigger than life, a man of unconquerable energy and incredible focus, one who attacked life and work with a ferocity that bordered on maniacal zeal. Scarcely a person who knew him does not describe Lombardi as driven – a man whose will dominated everything and everyone with whom he came in contact.

The question then is: What activated this driving force? Where did this man get his incredible energy, this courage, this almost superhuman impact that seemed to transform whatever and whomever he touched?

Family

It began in his childhood. Lombardi's parents were the incarnations of hardscrabble, bootstrapping New Yorkers. His father, Harry was an immigrant who earned his daily bread in the wholesale meat business. Harry literally wore the words 'work' and 'play' on his knuckles, evidence that, like his son, Vince, he saw life as difficult, but not without joy.

The work side, however, was characterized by strenuous labor, long hours, and intense competition. Life was hard, nothing was promised, and opportunities were few. There were no shortcuts for a large Italian, Catholic family from Sheepshead Bay in a New York world dominated by WASPs in business, politics, and culture.

While Lombardi's father, Harry, was a role model of the earn-every-buck capitalist, it was from Lombardi's mother, Matilda, that Vince learned the relentless perfectionism that marked his character. Called 'The Duchess' for her perfectionism and disciplinarian mien, Matilda was nothing less than a dominating figure, who would assign her children the most menial of duties, barking out directives and permitting not the slightest deviation from adherence to her instructions.

Early on, young Vince internalized the notion that authority figures had every right to exact total obedience from their subordinates, and perhaps more important, that no matter the seeming insignificance of a task, the only way to execute that duty was with perfection. In short, in all phases of life, doing things right was 'not a sometimes thing, but an all the time thing.'

Faith

As important as Lombardi's rearing was with regard to his respect for authority, commitment to hard work and pursuit of perfectionism, the calcifying force lay in his Christian faith. Vince Lombardi was not merely a Catholic, he was a daily communicant.

He was more comfortable with the saints of the church than with sinners in secular society. The Catholicism of his time seared into it followers the importance of submission to authority, an honest day's labor, and honoring God by offering no less than one's best.

During his coaching years, Lombardi quite literally preached to his players that they owed themselves, their teammates, and most important, God himself, nothing less than their very best. To offer an ounce less, to become comfortable with 'good enough,' to leave a job undone, was to cheat and dishonor the Creator in whose universe they were privileged to live.

All of this was underscored in Lombardi's days at Cathedral College of the Immaculate Conception, the prep school Lombardi attended in anticipation of becoming a priest, and where he first indicated a desire to lead, and at Fordham, a Catholic football power in New York.

It was at Fordham that the athletically limited Lombardi, through an unyielding attention to detail and perfection, developed into a first-rate lineman, a member of the famed 'Seven Blocks of Granite.' Here, again, Lombardi learned that life was hard, but success was attainable through hard work and an intense commitment to excellence.

Minority

But there's more. Had Vince Lombardi's first major coaching position been at the direction of a benign, soft-spoken leader, he may have seen and adopted a less demanding style, but Lombardi's first real taste of big-time coaching came at West Point.

He worked on the staff of the brilliant, autocratic, and absolutely legendary Earl Red Blaik, reinforcing the notion – modeled by 'The Duchess' – that to lead effectively, one had to be authoritarian, demanding, and unyielding. That was leadership. There was no other way.

Highly touted by Blaik, Lombardi went on to coach the offense of the New York football Giants. He labored brilliantly, but in obscurity.

As celebrated as triple threat halfback Frank Gifford was – a player much molded by Lombardi and after whom Paul Hornung was fashioned – the Giants were renowned for their defense. When Giants fans spoke of their heroes, they spoke of Sam Huff, Andy Robustelli, and members of the hangman defense, who stopped no one less than *the* Jim Brown – Jim Katcavage, Roosevelt Grier, and Dick Modzelewski.

What was missing from the then young Lombardi's life was the thing that psychological researchers often identify as among the most critical of all human needs: recognition. It was one thing to be a good son, solid football player, and outstanding coach. It was another to enjoy the recognition and confirmation of others, particularly in the form of career advancement. Lombardi received little of that.

He thirsted to prove himself as a head coach, but watched with pain as lesser lights advanced to head coaching positions in college and in the pros. The pain was intensified, because in the society of his era, Vince Lombardi was a minority.

He was a dark-skinned Italian, not unaccustomed to the dreaded 'N-word,' and as a minority, he had been left behind. Little wonder that Lombardi was way ahead of his time in relating to African-American players.

Yearning for an opportunity, he was passed over by the Air Force, Penn Washington, Wake Forest, and NFL teams. It seemed that in the WASPish world of big-time football, no one was willing to confer the title of head coach on a man whose name ended in a vowel. At 45, after serial disappointments and periods of depression, Lombardi got his opportunity. He was hired to coach the Green Bay Packers beginning in 1959.

To call it an opportunity is to stretch the meaning of the word. Vince Lombardi took over a team that had gone 1-10-1 the previous year, and had not had a winning season since 1947. But for Lombardi, a minority in his day, it was his first, and perhaps last, opportunity. God had opened a door and given his servant, Vincent, a test.

The test was not really about football. It was about character. The question was whether Lombardi could be true to the values of his youth, his faith, and his professional training, and turn this opportunity – as meager as it was – into success. Would he show his thankfulness by paying the price in energy and commitment to make the Green Bay Packers a success?

To fail in Green Bay would be a repudiation of everything he knew. It would certainly be a repudiation of the creed of his father, one that offered no excuse for not capitalizing on any opportunity, no matter its difficulty. It would most certainly repudiate the bedrock belief of his mother, that there were no menial tasks, only jobs that were to be done with excellence.

It would also repudiate his training in the Catholic Church, as well as educational institutions – that God calls and the servants answer with a faithfulness characterized by commitment. Still more, it would repudiate the life doctrine of Red Blaik, that football was a form of civilized war and there was no honorable alternative to victory.

Perhaps most painful of all, it would repudiate his own inner belief, that he – the squat little Italian, ever in an assistant's role – could be a successful head coach.

In that context, it was easy to understand why Lombardi all but abandoned his wife and children as he labored with maniacal dedication for the success of the Green Bay Packers. He had learned little about nurturing from his mother, and so, had little skill nurturing his alcoholically troubled wife and emotionally needy children.

Besides, the identity and worth of a man of his era resided in the nature and quality of his work. All this becomes evident when one reflects on the many aphorisms Lombardi used to spur his team on to success. Concepts such as courage, excellence, second effort, getting up when one is down, and running to win were not corny sayings to be trotted out in an effort to manipulate his players with a bit more zeal. They were doctrines by which one lived, and if one's calling was to play football, then it was on the gridiron that one was to live out these doctrines, and define one's worth by one's quest for excellence.

For Lombardi, being the boss was neither a privilege, nor a responsibility. It was a calling. He was hired to lead. He was morally obligated before God and humanity to lead men to victory on the football field. And because Lombardi's concept of leadership was burnished in the discipline of a Catholic education and West Point, it was the only way he led.

By Lombardi logic, he showed his love for his players not by nurturing them, encouraging them, and extending grace for their misdeeds, but by exacting greatness from them – by getting them to honor God by living out the external values of hard work and a pursuit of excellence.

When the success Lombardi sought so fervently arrived, however, it became the prison of his psyche. It drove him to ever higher levels of intensity simply to maintain it.

Unlike cool, ragingly successful Tom Landry, who coached the Dallas Cowboys brilliantly for 29 years, the seemingly indestructible Lombardi was burned out in less than a decade. After five NFL championships and nine straight winning seasons, Lombardi resigned as head coach of the Green Bay Packers in 1967.

Three years later, at 57 years of age, Vince Lombardi was dead.

It didn't seem fair. Independently wealthy, yet unable to anesthetize his drive, by 1970, Lombardi had taken over the football reins of the Washington Redskins and had driven

Profiles of Courage • VINCE LOMBARDI

Though he endorsed the change and believed it was best for everyone involved at the time, Lombardi clearly was moved at the press conference announcing that longtime assistant Phil Bengtson would become head coach for the 1968 season.

Pallbearers carry the casket of the late Vince Lombardi into St. Patrick's Cathedral on the day of the former Packer coach's funeral.

this perennial loser to a winning season in his first year. Championships now seemed imminent, but it was not to be.

Riddled with cancer, the light went out on September 3, 1970. Although the life force left Lombardi, the essence of the man was left behind in a way that not even he – who in his middle years had all but given up hope of ever being a major football head coach – could ever imagine. He also left us all a legacy of the *courage of his conviction*.

This chapter on the courage of Vince Lombardi, was written by David Claerbaut, author of many books, including, Bart Starr, When Leadership Mattered.

Arnie Herber

Hometown hero overcomes ridicule to become a star

Some of the Packers made fun of the part-Oneida Indian with his bushy hair and Native American features. They called him 'Dummy' and other heartless names, and they laughed at his hands that were so small, he couldn't even get his fingers on the laces of the football. He had to cradle the ball in his hand and heave it.

Yet this young man had enough inner strength and self-reliance to overcome the put-downs, ridicule, and physical limitations. One of the most unlikely stars of the Packers' legendary history was a hometown boy by the name of Arnie Herber.

Like Packer founder and coach of 31 years, Curly Lambeau, Herber grew up in Green Bay. Herber was a hometown boy who made good with the Packers, almost overnight, despite only one year of college experience. He had been a triple threat back in football, a high-scoring guard in basketball, and a weight man in track while at Green Bay West High School.

He attended the University of Wisconsin as a freshman, then transferred to Regis in Denver. He played only one season before the stock market crash caused Regis to suspend football.

Lambeau surprised everyone when he signed the 20-year-old Herber to a contract in 1930, since he had little college experience and most players had known him as the clubhouse handyman. Ironically, Herber would be a major factor in the championship years from 1933 through 1940.

The 5'-11", 208-pound Herber would lead the Packers to NFL championship games in 1936, 1938, and 1939, winning twice. The league's passing leader in 1932, 1934, and 1936, Herber could punt, run, and catch passes, but was best known for his arm strength.

Herber could throw a great distance, but his passes were not sharp and flat in trajectory as is synonymous with good passing. Herber's throws were more on the order of outfield flies. Star receiver Don Hutson would tell Herber where to throw. Hutson's incredible knack of timing and faking the secondary worked wonders. He was usually there when the ball came down. "Actually, the longest pass I ever threw in a game was 75 yards, against the St. Louis Gunners," Herber recalled. "Don Hutson caught the ball on the goal line."

Herber was already an established star when the fabled Don Hutson, fleet receiver from Alabama, entered the Packers' picture in 1935. The two, both destined for membership in the Pro Football Hale of Fame, quickly became an 'item,' without doubt the first great pass-catch team in the NFL annals.

Herber had smaller hands and fingers, which gave him a most unusual grip on the football. Instead of putting his entire hand around the end of the pigskin, with his fingers holding onto the laces and the thumb on the opposite side, he cradled the ball in his palms with his fingers and thumb on the stitches. Instead of throwing, he actually heaved the ball. With this rather unique passing technique, he was extremely accurate and could throw it a 'mile.'

At the finish of one of their championship seasons, the Packers went to Hollywood to make a movie. One sequence called for Herber to throw the ball from the 50-yard line and break a three-foot-square pane of glass which had been suspended from the crossbar between the goal posts. Arnie

PROFILES OF COURAGE • ARNIE HERBER

When he first joined the Packers in 1930, Herber had to have enough inner strength and self-reliance to overcome put-downs and ridicule from his teammates.   *Lefebvre photo*

took a few warm-up tosses and, on his first real attempt, hit the bulls-eye. But the director had failed to get the cameras rolling. He told Arnie he would have to do it again. Calmly, on his next toss, Herber duplicated the feat. That will give the younger fans, who never saw Herber throw a football, some idea of why Coach Curly Lambeau called him "the greatest long passer ever."

"There was a twist to that story that isn't generally known," Herber would explain later in his life. "After I had broken the pane twice from 50 yards out, they moved the camera into the end zone, for a close-up of the football shattering the glass. I wasn't going to be in the picture, so I stood about 10 feet away – and missed."

Herber had a rough time being accepted by some of the players. During his first season, some of the Packer veterans were almost cruel in their treatment of the hometown rookie. They nicknamed him 'Dummy.' Lambeau ordered this to stop. One veteran persisted within Lambeau's hearing and was immediately traded.

His teammates teased and called the young, bushy-haired Herber names during his rookie season, but they became awed by his passing skills later in his career.

As a teenager in Green Bay, Herber sold programs to watch the Packers play. He eventually attended tiny Regis College in Denver, but soon returned to Green Bay, where he worked as a handyman in the Packers' clubhouse.

One day, Lambeau, much to the amazement of the players, decided to give Herber a tryout. Some of the players still saw Herber, better known as 'Dummy,' as the boy who ran errands around the Packer camp.

Lambeau solved that one day by giving Herber the wrong time for the practice session. Then with Herber absent, Lambeau told the players, "Lay off the 'Dummy.' We're going to play football, and this kid is going to win with us. I'll punch the nose of the first man who forgets that."

Herber was the NFL passing leader in 1932, 1934, and 1936. His career record shows 410 completions for 6,741 yards. Handicapped by short fingers and pudgy hands, he gripped the ball with his thumb over the laces to prevent wobbling and impart spiraling action on the long arching throws for which he was famous.

While Herber was considered an outstanding passer in the 1930's, his statistics would not compare well to today's NFL quarterbacks. Although he was Green Bay's best passer, he averaged about 120 passes a season, less than ten per game. His passes accounted for 8,033 yards and almost 90 touchdowns; his best season coming in 1936 when he completed 77 passes for 1,239 yards and eleven touchdowns.

Here's how he remembers one of the games during his career in 1935. "I believe that half the people in Green Bay didn't realize what transpired in Wrigley Field in 1935 until they picked up the paper the next day. With less than three minutes to play, we were losing, 14-3. Everyone knew we had to pass after taking over the ball on our 35-yard line. We put Don Hutson on the flank and he broke between two defenders and scored, but the Bears still weren't worried. The only way we could win was to get the ball. On the first play after the kick-off, the Bears fumbled and we recovered on the Chicago 14. Three plays carried to the three and then it was Hutson again. With 10 seconds remaining, he sped straight down the field, quickly cut to his left, and I hit him for the winning touchdown.

"There was nobody in the league like Hutson. He had an uncanny change of pace and when you told him to be in a certain spot, he was always there."

Herber's nickname went from 'Dummy' to 'The Kid.' As respect and acceptance grew, they called him 'The Flash.' Nevertheless, he would later manage to get into Lambeau's doghouse. He continually fought a weight problem, which irritated Lambeau.

Then there was the 'accident' that was described by Gary D'Amato and Cliff Christly in their book, *Mudbaths and Bloodbaths.*

"When Herber was involved in an automobile accident on December 7, 1933, three days before the Packers met the

Bears at Wrigley Field, he suffered serious injuries, but it did little damage to his reputation. Herber was involved in the accident at 4:30 a.m. the Thursday before the game and was unable to play the following Sunday. He dislocated his right hip, injured his right forearm and sustained a four-inch laceration on the left side of his face when he drove into the rear of a truck near Green Bay."

Arnie was a Packer in an era when the quarterback was fair game, even after he threw the ball. This, added to the fact that he needed extra time for his receivers to get downfield for his long passes, meant that he took many fierce beatings. Yet, in his early years with the Packers, he never wore a helmet.

During the 1937 season, Arnie suffered a leg injury that sharply reduced his effectiveness. In 1938, a new passer, Cecil Isbell from Purdue, began alternating the Packer quarterback chores with Herber. After the 1940 season, Arnie retired.

Actually, Lambeau forced his retirement just before the start of the 1941 season, based on my research and interviews. Lambeau's second wife, Susan, whom he had divorced earlier that year, showed up in Green Bay eight months pregnant. Since he was convinced the child was not his because he had found evidence of her indiscretions in their home in LA, Lambeau put the word out that no one on the team could talk to her.

He refused to see her, even though Susan insisted the child was his. He denied it and said it was the result of her fooling around. It was Susan's intent to force Curly to pay child support as well as medical bills when it came time to deliver.

When she couldn't pay her rent at the Northland Hotel where she was living, she turned to Arnie's wife who took her in. When Curly found out, he insisted Herber ask Susan to leave their house so she could return to LA. Herber would have none of it, and he refused. Lambeau released him from the team, telling the *Press-Gazette* that Herber could not control his weight, so he had to cut him.

PROFILES OF COURAGE • ARNIE HERBER

Arnie Herber's passes were not pretty, but he could throw it a mile. He and the great Don Hutson hooked up on many long passes during the 1930s.

Four players from the championship era pose with Curly Lambeau and Red Smith at training camp in 1937. Arnie Herber and Mike Michalske are on the left, Milt Gantenbein and Hank Bruder on the right. *Lefebvre photo*

In the book, *Packer Legends in Facts*, where each season of the Packers is chronicled, it simply states in 1941, "Arnie Herber was released in a surprising move, just before the beginning of the regular season."

Herber, although only 31, had slowed down somewhat and did struggle with his weight. Lambeau knew he could release Herber because Cecil Isbell was going to be the number one passer, on the team anyway. Isbell had taken over Herber's spot as the Packer's primary passer, reducing his playing time. Nevertheless, it came as a surprise when the popular Herber, an eleven-year veteran, was cut just before the start of the season.

Four years later, the New York Giants, beset by the manpower problems of World War II, talked Herber into coming back. Arnie was by then 34 years old and had not thrown a football in three years when he reported to the Giants' summer camp. He had so much surplus weight that newspaper writers described him as a 'Tub o' Lard.' But he went to work with fierce diligence, and by the start of that season, was down to his playing weight of 210 pounds.

Author Don Smith would write about Herber's comeback with the Giants, "In a game against the Eagles in that 1944 season, Herber completed five to six passes for 114 yards and two touchdowns in the last six minutes of the game to give the Giants a 21-21 tie. The Giants startled the sports world that season with a complete turn-about of fortunes that brought them to the Eastern Division championship. A splendid defense that yielded only 75 points, a battering-ram fullback named Bill Pascal and one old man named Herber had made the New York victory possible. In the NFL title game against Arnie's old team, the Packers, the Giants lost, 14-7."

Smith also added, "The Giants slumped dismally in 1945, but Herber has his moments. The New Yorkers were trailing Philadelphia, 21-0, when Arnie entered the game in the third quarter. In the space of four minutes and 48 seconds, Herber exploded with three touchdown passes to an obscure end named Frank Liebel and then added a fourth to give the Giants a 28-21 victory. Playing in just the second half, Arnie completed 10 of 16 passes for 187 yards and the four touchdowns." (*The Coffin Corner*, Volume VI)

After his final retirement after the 1945 season, Herber returned to Green Bay where he ran a soft drink business with his brother. He died at the age of 59 in October 1969, just three years after his election to the Pro Football Hall of Fame. He was inducted into the Packer Hall of Fame in 1972, three years after his death.

As one Green Bay enthusiast once wrote, "Arnie Herber was the Babe Ruth of Pro Football. Like Babe, he specialized in the 'long ball,' was highly popular with the fans, and left a lasting mark on the sport he played." And all because he had the courage and nerve to overcome the ridicule and mockery from fellow Packers when he first joined the team.

Clark Hinkle

Brute force was his game

Clark Hinkle played fullback on offense and linebacker on defense for the Packers during the 1930's. Off the field, he was mild-mannered and soft-spoken. On the field, he was a raving madman, intent on inflicting bodily harm. Few Packers ever showed more courage on the field of play.

All through his 31 years as Packer head coach, Curly Lambeau had the uncanny skill of finding outstanding football players. In 1932, Lambeau found another key player, one who would go on to greatness as a Packer and also be inducted into the Pro Football Hall of Fame.

Hinkle was his name. Brute force was his game. He ran like a runaway truck, tackled with brute force, cried when the Packers lost, and once kicked the winning field goal with a deep gash exposing his shinbone.

Clarke Hinkle joined the Packers out of Bucknell College and played with them through 1941, when he went into the armed services in World War II. At 200 pounds, he was Green Bay's answer to the Bears' 238-pound Bronko Nagurski. During Hinkle's playing days (1932-41), players went both offense and defense. He played fullback and linebacker – usually the entire game.

Hinkle was not especially big at 5'-11", but he was one of the most bruising hitters, both rushing and tackling, in

1930's. "When he hit you," Ken Strong, legendary New York Giants' back, once said, "you knew you were being hit. Bells rang and you felt it all the way down to your toes."

"No one in the whole league bruised me more than Hinkle did," said John Sisk, who played halfback for the Bears in the midst of Hinkle's career. "After we had played the Packers, I'd be black-and-blue down to my toenails," Sisk recalled. "All I'd want was peace and quiet. Hinkle has a lot of leg action. I broke my shoulder twice trying tackle Hinkle."

Hinkle played linebacker on defense where his encounters with the Bears' Bronko Nagurski were nothing short of barbaric duels. Hinkle had the unique, if painful, distinction of being the only man ever to knock Nagurski out of the game.

It happened as the result of one of their frequent bone-shattering collisions, and in that particular one, 'The Bronk' came out of it with a broken nose and a broken rib. Hinkle and Nagurski both played fullback and linebacker, and they met head-on many times.

Perhaps their most resounding contact occurred in a game at Green Bay. In those days, punting a third down with long yardage was not uncommon. The Packers had the ball on their 20, third down and 14 to go. Hinkle ran to his right and Nagurski moved to meet him. Nagurski, in tackling or in blocking, rarely left his feet. On this occasion, Hinkle neared the sideline. Nagurski tired to block him out of bounds, but instead, Hinkle lowered his shoulder and smashed it into Nagurski's face. Hinkle ran into Nagurski and over him, stayed in bounds, and reached midfield for a first down before he was brought down from behind.

They didn't wear face masks or guards in those days. Nagurski had to be helped from the field. He had suffered a broken nose, a broken and some bruised ribs, a fractured hip, and a wrenched shoulder.

Hinkle recalled the hit, "I saw Nagurski coming over to really nail me to the cross, but I had the ball and knew what I was going to do. So before I went out of bounds at the side-

PROFILES OF COURAGE • CLARK HINKLE

(Left) Clarke Hinkle has been called the finest all-around player in Packer history. A punishing runner, he was a fine defensive back, better than average passer, and a great place kicker and punter.

Lefebvre photo

(Right) Hinkle ran like a runaway truck, tackled with brute force, cried when the Packers lost, and once kicked the winnng field goal with a deep gash exposing his shin bone.

line, I cut back in on him and caught him square with my shoulder and head. He knocked me back, pretty near five yards. I sat there for a second because it really shook me up. Then I looked over to old 'Bronk' and his nose was all over his face and he was in helluva shape. Nagurski had a broken nose and later found he had a broken rib, too. George Halas was really mad about it, and he said I played Bronk dirty. I don't know how he got that. I was carrying the ball. I couldn't do anything dirty."

After their playing days were over, Hinkle and Nagurski remained friends. Hinkle said, "Nagurski was a great guy and we have become good friends. He was my presenter when I was inducted into the Hall of Fame."

Hinkle rarely missed a play, let alone a game, because of injury. Authors Gary D'Amato and Cliff Christl wrote of one of the times it happened. It was in 1941, when the Bears' fullback, Bill Osmanski, caught Hinkle with his cleats, opening a gash on his shin that exposed the bone. Hinkle stayed on the field for two or three plays, but then called a time out and jogged to the sideline to get the wound dressed. Curly Lambeau, who berated him for wasting a time out, greeted him.

"I said to Lambeau, 'Listen, my shinbone's showing.'" Hinkle said in *The Game That Was*, "I came over to get a bandage on it because, you know, it kind of makes me sick to look at my shinbone."

Hinkle not only went back into the game, but he kicked a 38-yard field goal, giving the Packers what proved to be the winning points in a 16-14 victory. After the game, there were no taxis to be found on the deserted streets around Wrigley Field, so Hinkle walked the fifteen blocks to the team hotel.

Actually, there was no part of football at which Hinkle did not excel. He blocked savagely, both on runs and protecting the passer. He was the workhouse runner and the leading ground gainer of his day. He carried the ball 1,171 times in ten league seasons and gained 3,860 yards, which is still the Packers' sixth-best career rushing total.

Hinkle still is tied for first with Jim Taylor in the Packer record book for the most seasons leading the team in rushing – seven. While he ran with brute force, Hinkle was an excellent faker. He frequently hit the line without the ball and drew the defense to himself, while Arnie Herber, and later, Cecil Isbell gained time to fade back for a long pass to Don Hutson.

Hinkle caught the ball well and he could also throw it adequately in the Packers' old-time version of the option pass. He punted and he kicked extra points and field goals. On defense, he was an integral part of Green Bay's answer to the opponents' runs and passes or both.

Hinkle's dedication to football and to the Packers was legendary. Lambeau could get him fired up before a game, but Hinkle was so emotional he would sometimes sit by his locker and weep after a loss. "I've never known a man who wanted to win like 'Hink' did," said a teammate. "Before a game he would get glassy-eyed, he'd be so fired up and eager to play. After the game, if we lost, he's sit at his locker and cry like a baby. He didn't know how to lose." (from *What a Game They Played*, by Richard Whittingham)

Although Hinkle would be one of Lambeau's toughest, most productive players for nearly ten years, the two were never close. Hinkle would say about Lambeau, "I never liked him, but he was paying me and I gave him a thousand percent every time I played football for him. There is one thing I do respect about Lambeau. Whenever we went out on the road, he'd make us wear suits, coats and ties. If we were in Green Bay, he wouldn't let us smoke in public because the people might think less of us.

When we would leave Green Bay on the train, we had two Pullmans and a dining car. We'd stay in the finest hotels on the road, and he'd sign the check so we could eat at the hotel. He wanted us to get the proper food, and he was trying to project the image that we were educated people who happened to be playing sports." (from *Vagabond Halfback* by Ralph Hickok)

Hinkle had a clean-cut, rather youthful-looking face, but

on the field he took on a ferocious, wild, savage look. He converted from mild-mannered and quiet into a football brute.

Hinkle backed up the line furiously on defense. A Green Bay linesman of the day recalled: "If the line was doing well in a game and stopping all the play, Hinkle would go crazy. 'Come on you guys,' he'd tell us, 'let him through on the next play and give me a chance. I want to hit somebody.'"

During his ten seasons (1932 – 1941) as a Packer, Hinkle displayed his versatility, totaling over 3,800 yards running, doing most of the team's punting, kicking 26 field goals, 28 extra points, catching 50 passes for nine touchdowns, scoring 43 total touchdowns, and completing nearly 50 percent of his passes.

In their book, authors Gary D'Amato and Cliff Christl related a story about when well-known sports writer, Paul Zimmerman, watching a Packer game film showing Hinkle performing on the field. Zimmerman was actually watching the old game film for an article he was writing for *Sports Illustrated* in 1989. He was researching for material on Packer great, Don Hutson, and Bear Star, Bronko Nagurski. While viewing the film, Zimmerman was greatly impressed with Hinkle.

"My impression was that Hinkle was a lot better than people gave him credit for," Zimmerman said. "He was a well-kept secret in Green Bay. He made the all-pro teams because he was a dominating back, but he never got the publicity or notoriety that Nagurski got. Bronko was a great name, and Nagurski was bigger.

"But Hinkle, shit, he was an iron man. He played like a fucking maniac. So, yeah, I think he was every bit as good. I saw him make a tackle, and he went flying. You saw a blur coming into the screen, like he was possessed. And he smashed some guy out of bounds and into the seats. Jesus!"

"Clarke Hinkle was the greatest all-around football player of all time," said Charles 'Buckets' Goldenberg, admittedly a slightly prejudiced witness who played guard with the Packers throughout Hinkle's career. " He didn't hit

PROFILES OF COURAGE • CLARK HINKLE

Hinkle in a publicity shot in the 1930s.

Off the field, Hinkle was mildmannered and soft-spoken. On the field, he was a raving madman. Few Packers showed more courage on the field.

...and in his last season, 1941.

Hinkle as a rookie in 1932...

as hard straight on as Bronko Nagurski. He didn't have the 'Nag's' size, but he could do so many things, and do them all well."

Those who evaluate NFL talent agreed with Goldenberg. Hinkle was elected to the prestigious Pro Football Hall of Fame in 1964 and the honored Packer Hall of Fame in 1972.

After his retirement from the Packers in 1941, and his discharge from the military services after the war, Hinkle returned to Ohio and became a salesman. He died on November 9, 1988, in Steubenville, Ohio, at the age of 79.

During Hinkle's ten seasons, the Packers were 80-35-4. Along with Hall-of-Famers from that era, such as Don Hutson, Arnie Herber, and Cecil Isbell, the Packers were the NFL's best. Hinkle had few peers in the NFL during the period he played with the Packers, and few can claim to have displayed more raw courage on the playing field.

Tony Canadeo
A hero for all seasons

He wasn't thinking about his playing days with the Packers as he drifted in and out of consciousness in the ambulance that was driving at breakneck speed. Burning up with a fever and hallucinating, the thoughts of his All-Pro, eleven-year career as a Packer were the furthest things from his mind.

Right now, his only thoughts were to somehow stay alive until he got to the hospital 200 miles away. Tony Canadeo didn't know it on that cold winter day in 1972, but his kidneys were in the process of shutting down. He was sick, terribly sick. Another day to two without proper medical care, and he never would have had the chance to receive his induction into the honored Pro Football Hall of Fame.

When Tony Canadeo played for the Packers during the 1940's and early 1950's, he was a popular hero to all the fans who followed the team. He went on to become one of the most admired figures in the Packers' history.

But now, having felt ill for weeks, the 53-year-old former Packer great and running back and his family suddenly realized he was fighting for his life. Recollections of that desperate trip on a cold, windy, snowy day to Milwaukee are still fresh in the minds of his wife and son, Bob. "I was in the ambulance with him and he was 'out of it.' He was hallucinating all the way to Milwaukee while they had him on oxygen. The roads were awful. It was one of those blustery, rainy, snowy Januarys," recalled Ruth.

As they pulled into the emergency entrance at County Hospital, the ambulance was met by a group of nurses and doctors. Canadeo looked terrible and he was still hallucinating. They started the peritoneal dialysis immediately.

That went on for two days while Ruth slept on a couch in the waiting room. When she was allowed to visit Tony at his bedside, he was still feverish and hallucinating, seeing snakes coming out of the walls of his room. A priest gave him Last Rites. Ruth took catnaps in the waiting room, clutching her rosary and saying prayers. "You beg and beg. You finally get to the point where you say, 'It's in your hands, you do what you think is best,'" she recalled.

Tony's best friend, Dick Bourguignon, was in a hotel in Florida the night he received the phone call that Tony had been taken to County Hospital in Milwaukee and was very ill. Dick left the hotel and walked the beach until daylight, praying and pleading with God that his friend would recover.

While he was praying for Canadeo's recovery, Bourguignon's thoughts drifted back to Tony's playing days in Green Bay. Canadeo excelled in almost every phase in the game of football while playing for the Packers from 1941 through 1952. He played both offense and defense, rushed with the football, and threw passes. He was one of the most versatile players in the history of the Packers.

During his eleven years with the Packers, interrupted by military service from 1944-45, Canadeo rushed for 4,197 yards on 1,025 carries, caught 69 passes for 579 yards, scored 186 points on 31 touchdowns, completed 105 passes for 1,642 yards and 16 touchdowns, punted 45 times for a 37-yard average, intercepted nine passes and returned them 129 yards, returned 45 punts for an 11.3 average, and ran back 71 kickoffs for 1,626 yards and a 22.9-yard average.

He became only the third 1,000-yard rusher in league history when he gained 1,052 yards in 1949. Canadeo is one

PROFILES OF COURAGE • TONY CANADEO

Tony Candaeo would become one of the most admired figures in the Packers' history.
Packer Hall of Fame photo

of 20 Packers enshrined in Canton, Ohio, and one of only five Packers to have his jersey, Number 3, retired, joining Don Hutson, 14; Bart Starr, 15; Ray Nitschke, 66; and Reggie White, 92.

Bourguignon remembers Tony fell in love and married a Green Bay girl, Ruth, in 1943. They had five children. He lived his entire life in Green Bay after signing with the Packers as a seventh-round draft choice in 1941.

Meanwhile, after he was admitted to the hospital on that-near fatal Day in 1972, Canadeo began to slowly come around. However, his kidneys had shut down. When he was told his kidneys could no longer function normally and he was shown the dialysis machine, he looked at it, broke down and wept.

As soon as he was stabilized, he was transferred to nearby Veterans Hospital where he began the arduous seven-hour dialysis treatments. Within a day, it began to sink in just what it would mean to live the rest of his life getting seven-hour dialysis treatments several times a week. When the medical staff told him that after his release, he would need to come to the hospital twice a week for treatment, he couldn't believe what they were telling him.

Once a strong, energetic athlete, he now felt like an invalid. Although he went back to work after a few months, the trips back and forth, twice a week, and the seven hours on the dialysis machine, made him feel much less a man than at any time before in his life.

After seven months of the dialysis routine, the mental strain became almost unbearable. Tony begged for the risky surgery of a kidney transplant. He wanted to end the treatments and the only way to do that was with a transplant.

After the final decision to go ahead with the surgery, the search for a qualified donor began. His three son's, Bob, Tom, and Tony, Jr., all went through extensive testing to determine if they would qualify as kidney donors. Ruth asked to be tested also. Canadeo kept insisting he didn't want any of the boys or Ruth to donate their kidney, but there were no other options. It turned out that Bob's was the match.

Dr. Myron Kauffman performed the surgery at seven o'clock in the morning on the first of August in 1972. Shortly after noon, Dr. Kauffman came to the waiting room to say the surgery had been a success.

"It seems to me that I started bawling," Ruth said.

A day after the surgery, Dr. Kauffman commented to Tony that his kidneys had been encased in a sea of scars from playing football for nearly 20 years, and that he really put him to some hard work to get the kidneys out, much more so than during the same procedure on other patients.

Tony looked at Dr. Kauffman, grinned and said, "If you haven't peed red, you haven't played in the NFL."

Initially after his transplant, Tony did well. He went home, but several weeks later he came back to visit Dr. Kauffman with a high fever and feeling ill. Tony's pathology results had elements suggesting a rejection. It was not a classic rejection, but it was enough for Dr. Kauffman to treat him for a rejection episode. Tony said to Dr. Kauffman, "Whatever you say, Coach, that's what we're going to do."

Dr. Kauffman recalled, "One of the things that I remember very well about Tony is that he always called me 'Coach.'"

Canadeo was readmitted for the biopsy and treatment of rejection. He became very depressed. Throughout most of his initial post-operative course, Tony had been popular among the doctors, nurses and the rest of the hospital staff because he had been so upbeat and cheerful.

But he was depressed about this latest setback. Tony was so down, that one Sunday afternoon, Dr. Kauffman took him to his house to watch the Packers on television, just to get him out of the hospital and help get his mind off of it. Thirty years later, Dr, Kauffman said, "We subsequently became good friends. To make a long story short, his kidney function came back to normal."

With the bitter memory of his illness fading with time, the strong support of his family during that time, and the recognition he would receive, now took over. Fully recovered, and back on the job by January of 1973, Canadeo was invited to Appleton to receive the prestigious Red Smith Award.

As he stood up and walked to the podium, he was given a standing ovation that lasted over one minute. He told them he was overwhelmed. He said how fortunate he felt to be there and illustrated his good fortune with an analogy, "They say you have to have a great defense to win in pro football. About a year ago, I found out what my defense was…it was comprised of my faith in God, my family, and a lot of great friends who had the knack of being around when I needed them."

Tony continued, "Many times I despaired, but that's when you need your faith in God, your family and friends. My family never gave me a chance to be alone. My friends were always calling, asking me what they could do. In an illness like I had, the guys who succumb to despair are the ones who are alone. I was never alone."

As he left the podium and returned to his seat, he received another standing ovation, even longer and louder than the first one.

Within days of that heartwarming experience he would receive another as he was inducted into the Pro Football Hall of Fame. When Canadeo first received word of this, he couldn't believe he would be enshrined with the very best professional football players and coaches in the long, illustrious history of the game.

Canadeo chose his best friend, Dick Bourguignon, to introduce him. Each inductee had someone who meant a great deal to them make a formal introduction before making their acceptance speech. In his introduction speech, Dick said Canadeo was, "…an outstanding and complete football player; he could block, kick, pass, and above all, he was a tremendous runner. While at Gonzaga University, he gained the name 'Gray Ghost of Gonzaga.' He was not tricky, but very quick, and most of all, he's all heart."

A former teammate was asked to recall his impressions of Canadeo when he was playing halfback for the Green Bay Packers. "If you want Tony described in a nutshell, I'd say this: Tony Canadeo looked less like a football player than any other man on the team," the man said.

"He wasn't fast. He wasn't big. He wasn't elusive like a lot of runners. He wasn't really powerful. But when Tony put that ball under his arm, he was a wild man. Tony was all desire. He was fired up. That was what made him great; because he didn't have the natural ability of some of the others."

As Tony stood at the podium, clinging to his miniature bronze bust that would be displayed in the Hall, Ruth's eyes welled up as she reflected, "I thought daylight would never come, in what we had gone through. And then, here he is, up there giving his speech. I thought, 'God is good!'"

One of Canadeo's major accomplishments that put him into the Pro Football Hall of Fame took place in 1949. Lloyd Larson, then sportswriter for the *Milwaukee Sentinel*, wrote about Canadeo in one of his columns in September of 1949, "This great crowd pleaser and his sterling deeds is more remarkable when you consider his size and years of service in the toughest physical contact business imaginable. He's small, as pros go, and he's been in the league for seven seasons, a long, long time as measured in the postgraduate circuit. The answer may be that Tony personifies what many claim to be the basic element in keeping up football success – the combination of heart and terrific desire."

It was basically this desire that carried Tony to a *signature season* and a most remarkable feat in 1949. The Packers, 2-9, flew to Detroit to play the Lions, 3-8, on December 11, in the last game of the year. It was Tony's last chance to break the 1,000-yard mark. He got up that Sunday morning and looked out his hotel window to see that it was raining – not a good day for running the football.

The playing field was so dark, the lights were turned on at the start of the game. Only 12,576 fans, the smallest attendance on record for a Lions game, bothered to show up to watch two last-place teams play in miserable weather. With support from his line and blocking backs, Tony managed to slosh his way through the rain and mud to gain 70 very

PROFILES OF COURAGE • TONY CANADEO

Canadeo on a sprint against the Los Angeles Rams at the Los Angeles Coliseum in 1946. It was the last game of the season won by the Rams, 38-17.
Packer Hall of Fame photo

PROFILES OF COURAGE • TONY CANADEO

Tony Canadeo finally got his victory at Wrigley Field in his last game there in 1952. The Packers defeated the Bears 41-28.

Canadeo Collection photo

tough yards and go over the 1,000 mark to break Van Buren's old record of 1,008.

He finished the season with 1,052 yards in 208 attempts for an amazing 5.1 yards per carry average. His outstanding accomplishment was somewhat overshadowed by Steve Van Buren, who about an hour later that day, shattered his own old rushing record and finished ahead of Tony in the NFL rushing standings with 1,146 yards. In spite of Canadeo's amazing feat, the Packers lost to the Lions, 21-7.

Canadeo's rushing yardage put him into a select group of only three players in NFL history, at that point to have gained over 1,000 yards in one season – Beattie Feathers, Steve Van Buren and himself. To join this group at this time in the history of the NFL would be akin to being among the first to hit 60 home runs in a season, or to be one of the first few to break the four-minute mile.

After the 1949 season, Canadeo was named to the prestigious United Press All-Pro First Team. Canadeo was, indeed, a star; the only one that the Packers had at that time. He was not only a star performer on the field, but he was also the Packers' leading man off the field. He spoke at numerous school functions, church groups, the Packer Quarterback and Alumni groups and anywhere he was asked to appear. And he spoke not just in Green Bay, but elsewhere in the state, too.

However, when the 1950 season opened, new coach Gene Ronzani, who had replaced Curly Lambeau, switched Canadeo from halfback to fullback. Ronzani said he wanted younger, faster halfbacks. He felt Canadeo had 'lost a step.' At 190 pounds, Canadeo was not exactly built for the pounding a fullback takes. Never a complainer, Canadeo accepted the change and was determined to make the best of it.

Canadeo's ground-gaining totals dropped, even though he led the team in total rushing attempts. His rushing attempts and yardage dropped even further in 1951, but he became one of the Packers' leading receivers as Ronzani built his offense around the passing game. In 1952, his last season, Canadeo rushed for a total of 191 yards, and his pass receptions fell off as well.

However, he did manage to surpass Clark Hinkle as the Packers' career rushing leader, a record Canadeo held until Jimmy Taylor passed him in the mid-1960's. Canadeo was given tribute at the end of the 1950 season by the Quarterback Club in Green Bay. In his typical, self-effacing, humble demeanor, Tony said he would have gladly exchanged that with the great fullback, Clark Hinkle, since he was a much better runner than himself."

One of Canadeo's most memorable games came against the Packers' archrivals, the Bears, in 1952, his last season. Having grown up in Chicago, it had always been his dream to beat the Bears on their home field, his beloved Wrigley Field, where he had watched so many football games as a kid. After ten seasons of play as a Packer, he had never achieved this.

In early November, he got his last chance. Rushing and blocking with a passion, Tony led the team in rushing that day, and the Packers won, 41-28. After eleven years, Canadeo finally had his victory at Wrigley Field.

At the end of the game, the Packers' Washington Serini, a former Bear, started yelling to the team in the locker room to quiet down. Holding the ball that had been used in the final play of the game aloft, he said, "Hold it a minute! We're going to give this ball to Tony Canadeo. Today was his last Bears' game."

Everyone applauded.

Not long after that, Tony came into the room and Serini made the presentation to Tony, saying, "…in remembrance of your last Bears' game, and it was a great one!"

"It is improbable that this could have been matched, drama and where," wrote *Press-Gazette* reporter Lee Remmel. "Canadeo stood there with his teammates crowded around him, blood streaming from a cut under his right eye and another on his forehead, and unashamed tears ran down his cheeks. He, for a time, was unable to respond coherently, but finally he choked out in a cracked voice between sobs, 'Well, I said we are going to beat them today. My last year.'"

A few years ago, I was fortunate enough to write a book about the life of Canadeo. Tony was my Packer hero when I was a youngster. While spending week after week in Green Bay, I spent hours with Tony at his house, interviewed dozens of his former teammates, numerous associates, physicians, friends and family.

After finishing the book, I had seen the man's entire life. I studied it, researched it, and talked to Tony at length, many times. I also interviewed his family, friends, and former teammates and associates. A new kind of hero emerged different from those faded, illusionary memories of mine. I came to the realization that real heroes are shaped by what happens to them in everyday life – not just on some sports field.

What stands out most to me, was that Tony, even though he was a star and played an important role with the Packers, was a down-to-earth guy. He had a good sense of humor and a large dose of humility. He could be critical, but he always supported the coach. What really struck me, was how many friends and others adored him.

During my research for the book, there were endless stories of Canadeo's life-long generosity as well as his intense competitive spirit on the field. A former teammate from the late 1940's, Nolan Luhn, recalled the 1949 season, with the Packers winning only two games. "Everybody was thinking, 'Let's get this season over.' We went through earlier practices in pretty good shape, and then the coaches worked us a little extra hard. But Tony was doing his best to keep us up. I remember, we went to Chicago and got beat. We went back to the dressing room and Tony finally spoke up…he said we went out there and busted our rears and got beat. Tony then broke down and cried. I'll never forget that incident."

When football was over for Canadeo, it was over. He retired after the 1952 season. He had played with the throttle wide open, and when he decided to move on with his

PROFILES OF COURAGE • TONY CANADEO

In a special pre-game ceremony, Canadeo was given a "retirement" party, before meeting the Dallas Texans at City Stadium on a cold November day in 1952. Tony's jersey #3 was retired and Packer captain and close friend of Tony's, Bob Forte (left) makes the retirement official. Head coach Gene Ronzani looks on. Bobby Dillon can be seen far right. The Packers won 42-14 and Canadeo scored two touchdowns — his last as a Packer.
Canadeo Collection photo

Earl Gillespie (left) congratulates Canadeo during a special ceremony before the last home game in 1952 that was declared "Tony Canadeo Day." Gillespie was the popular radio play-by-play broadcaster for the Packers and had known Tony for years, becoming good friends during and after his football playing days.
Earl Gillespie Collection photo

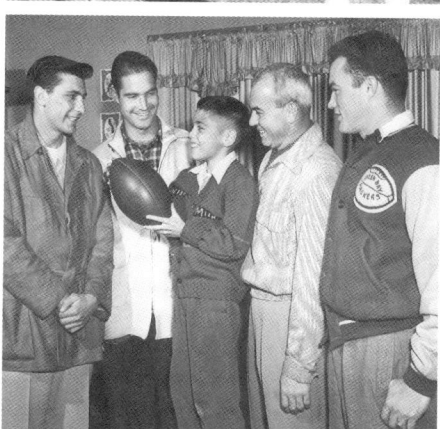

A 12-year old polio victim, Larry Bero, received a Packer football from (L-R) Babe Parilli, Tobin Rote, Tony and Fred Cone a few days before the Dallas Texans game in Green Bay.
Canadeo Collection photo

PROFILES OF COURAGE • TONY CANADEO

Tony shares a laugh with Vince and Marie Lombardi at a get together after a Packer game. Tony and Ruth were close friends of the Lombardis.
Stephen Schmidt photo, Canadeo collection

Tony became a good friend and confidant of Vince Lombardi. Shown here in 1970 are: (L-R) Tony, Dick Bourguignon, Vince and Jake Stathas.
Canadeo Collection photo

PROFILES OF COURAGE • TONY CANADEO

In the nine seasons as a Packer television color man, Canadeo had blossomed into one of pro football's better analysts. He learned to anticipate quarterback moves with frequency most opposition defense would envy.

Tony and Ray Scott became good friends during the nine years they telecast the Packer games together during the Packer glory years of the '60s.

life, he was ready. He had begun to build a career outside of football the year before he retired. He became a successful salesman for a steel company. After his retirement from football, Canadeo was also a color commentator for TV broadcasts of Packer games. It was a role that included teaming with Ray Scott during the franchise's 'Glory Years,' 1959-1967.

Shortly after his retirement as a player, Canadeo was invited to serve on the Packer Board of Directors, where he would serve for 38 years – from 1955 to 1993. A few years later, he became a member of the board's executive committee. It was while in this position that Canadeo also played a vital role in the selection and hiring of Vince Lombardi.

Late in his life, Canadeo suffered from skin cancer, and from his playing career, had problems with his lower legs, back and shoulder. Tony Canadeo, Jr., remembered his father having at least three surgeries in four years to fuse vertebrae in his back. However, Canadeo rarely betrayed the pain he suffered. He was supposed to be in a wheelchair for a few years, but refused to use one and was embarrassed he needed a walker to help his football-ravaged legs.

His health continued to deteriorate, and Tony died during his last of many trips to the hospital in late November, 2003, at the age of 84. His last words to his beloved wife, Ruthie, after he had fallen on his way to the bathroom and she was helping him up were, "I'm sorry." Seconds later, he passed away.

At his funeral mass, his son, Bob, and others considered the day a celebration of his life. The service focused on Canadeo's attitude toward life, family, faith and the importance of keeping a sense of humor. Not much was mentioned about his football accomplishments. That's the way Canadeo would have wanted it.

Father Getchel, who officiated at the funeral, told the gathering, "Tony went out of his way for other people. He cared about other people. He was concerned about other people. He loved the people around him very much. He would do anything he possibly could do for you. That's a great example of the Christian life."

His son Bob, who donated a kidney to Tony back in 1972, gave the eulogy. He recalled one occasion when, as a child, his Dad gave him some sound advice, "I was sitting up in my room and was feeling sad about something. I don't remember much about the conversation, but I do remember he said: 'Son, everyone in this world has a cross to bear. It's out duty to pick up that cross each and every day as best we can.'"

Canadeo certainly had his crosses to bear later in his life. After his near-death experience when his kidneys gave out, his body began to gradually wear out from the pounding he had taken playing football those many years. He suffered from constant, severe back pain and legs that no longer worked. He underwent repeated back surgeries and lesser operations for skin cancer. His shoulders locked up so tight,he couldn't comb his hair or put a on a coat without help.

But through it all, family and friends said, Canadeo remained upbeat, never took himself too seriously, and never lost his sense of humor. I experienced the same thing with Tony during my many interviews, our lunch's together at Eve's, and at book signings. He was warm, friendly, and cracked jokes with people who came up and asked him to autograph copies of our book, *In Search of a Hero – The Life and Times of Tony Canadeo.*

Ruth's brother, Father Toonen, who had given Canadeo Last Rites back in 1972, said in his speech at the funeral, "When a situation came up where he didn't know just exactly what to say or do, he'd say, 'When in doubt, punt.' It was his way of saying, 'Don't quit on this.' One thing about him, he was never one to quit. What he was saying was, 'Let's get the ball up in the air again, and we'll get back and get another chance. When it comes around again, we'll do better.'"

Tony Canadeo could certainly be considered a hero in terms of how he lived his life, and he will go down as one of the most affable and decent men to ever play for the

Packers. Certainly, no man has ever given more loyalty and service and lived an exemplary lifestyle.

While he was a proven star on the playing field, the character he displayed during his entire life was the more remarkable feature of Canadeo. What he portrayed was the essence of a life of courage, made by determining and identifying characteristics that, as it turned out, reached far beyond the restricted boundaries of the football field.

PROFILES OF COURAGE • TONY CANADEO

Tony and Ruth with their children. Front row: Tony Jr., Nancy, Mary Kay. Back row: Bob and Tom.
Chamberlin in 2001 photo, Canadeo collection

Tony and Ruth, his loving wife of nearly 60 years, in one of their most recent photos.
Chamberlin in 2001 photo, Canadeo collection

Bob Mann

The first African-American to play for the Packers. It took a unique courage to break the 'color barrier'

When former Packer receiver Bob Mann died in October 2006, at the age of 82, it brought back fond memories for me of his remarkable, but all too brief, NFL career. The quiet-spoken, mild-mannered Mann joined the Packers late in the 1950 season. When he played in the last three games that year, he made Packer history by becoming the first African-American to play in a league game for the Packers.

He also set receiving records in his short, three-year tenure, and his 208 receptions in his five full seasons, 1948-53, ranked second in the NFL during that period. Surprisingly enough, the signing, the Saturday after Thanksgiving, of this truly gifted receiver by Packer coach Gene Ronzani didn't spark much press in 1950. As a youngster, I remember reading small articles in the Green Bay *Press-Gazette* and the *Milwaukee Journal*, and they did not play up his signing. In fact, I saved the clippings for years.

Not only was Mann the first Black to ever play for the Packers, but he had also been an All-American at the University of Michigan in 1947, had caught 33 passes in 1948, and had led the NFL with 66 receptions with the Detroit Lions in 1949.

Although the Packers had had two other Black players on the team in 1950, both had been cut before the season started. But not before they caused a flap before being released. Some of the White Packers complained, and even refused to have their picture taken with the Black players, according to Art Daley, who was the sports editor for the Green Bay *Press-Gazette* during that time. It took a different kind of courage for a Black to play professional sports during that period.

Mann recalled the day he walked into the all-White Packer locker room as being an "unusual situation, I guess." Jerry Poling wrote in his book, *Downfield*, that walking into all-White professional and social situations had become almost commonplace for Mann. He was used to it, but his new Packer teammates weren't.

"I remember the first time he walked into the locker room. There was silence," said Clayton Tonnemaker, a rookie center on the 1950 team. "We knew he was coming, but in that locker room, it was a big deal, like Jackie Robinson joining the Brooklyn Dodgers. We had a lot of Southern guys on the team, a lot from Texas. They had never played with a Black before."

Keep in mind, this was just a few years after Jackie Robinson, a friend of Mann's, broke the 'color barrier' in baseball's major leagues by playing for the Brooklyn Dodgers in 1947. When Blacks were integrating sports, the media often would single out Black athletes in their reports, referring to them as Negro, Colored or Black.

Daley told me, "Bob played five seasons in Green Bay and he was an eye-opener for this local sportswriter back then since I had never even known an African-American until Mann came along. It was an education I would never forget. Mann recognized this 'country boy' right away and cautioned me against using the word 'Colored' in referring to Black players in my newspaper. "We want to be called Negroes."

Poling would write, "Mann was just one of seventeen Blacks out of a population of 52,735 in Green Bay, according

PROFILES OF COURAGE • BOB MANN

Bob Mann was the first African-American to play in a league game for the Packers in 1950. He was inducted into the Packer Hall of Fame in 1988. He was a gifted receiver for the Pack from 1950-1953.

Packer Hall of Fame photo

to the 1950 U.S. Census. Packer players say the only other Green Bay Black they remember was a man who shined shoes in a local hotel.

Mann was eventually accepted by his teammates, and while he may not have felt at home, he was made to feel as comfortable as possible in a white city, on a white team. He said, 'The Green Bay people were nice and warm. They all talked football. It was a wonderful football town. I have no complaints.'"

Mann told Art Daley he never was denied service in any Green Bay restaurant or hotel because of his color. Mann stayed at the Northland Hotel in Green Bay, along with many other Packers.

When he first got to Green Bay, Mann said he was treated, well despite joining a team that had never had an African-American player. "I remember walking into the dressing room," Mann once said of his first day. "It was quiet, but everyone was friendly. Almost all the guys came up and greeted me. I think Tony Canadeo was one of the first guys. I remember going out and having Tobin Rote throw me some passes. The first pass he overthrew, and I caught it with one hand. He said, 'Nice catch.' I knew from his expression, he was pleased to have someone else to throw to."

Mann "…was a popular guy. He came out with us at night after the ball games. We'd go someplace and dance. All the wives would dance with him. He was well accepted by everyone," said Dick Wildung, a tackle and captain of the team.

Mann joined the Packers during a time when Blacks were still coping with unjust racial barriers throughout the nation. Art Daley, editor during that time, recalled a few discrimination incidents, "The Packers were playing the Texans (not yet the Cowboys), in Dallas in 1952, and on nights before games, the Packers always practiced. I remember walking off the field with Bob and he couldn't ride the team bus and had to take a cab to his hotel. I yipped a few expletives but Mann didn't seem too perturbed, explaining, 'That just politics.'"

While the people of Green Bay accepted Mann, it was often a different story on the road where segregation raised its ugly head. When the Packers went to play in Baltimore in 1953, Mann wasn't allowed to stay with the team at the Whites-only hotel; he was sent to a Black hotel.

Mann recalled the Packers playing the Colts in Baltimore, "I was allowed in the team hotel for a meeting, and afterwards, I walked out of the hotel with Dick Afflis to catch a cab to my hotel. The cab driver said, 'I can't take him,' pointing to me. Dick grabbed that poor driver by the shirt and told him, 'You take him where he wants to go!' and he did." Dick later became widely known as the wrestler, 'Dick the Bruiser.'

After those two very good seasons with the Lions, while in the middle of a contract dispute, Detroit traded Mann to the New York Yanks for future-Hall-of-Fame quarterback Bobby Layne. Mann never played a down for the Yankees and was cut loose in the middle of the 1950 season.

Desperate to put some life into his Packers' offense, Gene Ronzani signed Mann. Before Ronzani took over from Curly Lambeau as head coach of the Packers in 1950, the club had never had an African-American player, even though the 'color barrier' had been broken years before in the NFL.

While he did not make an impact in the last few games of 1950 season, the slightly built Mann would lead the Packers with 50 receptions in 1951. He became only the second receiver in Packer history to catch as many as 50 passes in a season, and finally finished fourth in the NFL, overall.

To put this accomplishment in perspective, the only other receiver to turn that trick in the Packers' previous 30 seasons had been the legendary Don Hutson.

Ronzani took advantage of the 5'-11", 175-pound Mann's unique ability to regularly fake out defenders in order to get open and and his ability to catch almost anything thrown in his direction in 1951. Ronzani designed a wide open passing offense with quarterbacks Tobin Rote and Bobby Thomason throwing enough to set Packer passing records that stood for nearly 20 years.

The Packers started out well that year, beginning with a 3-2 record, but then lost their last seven games to finish 3-9. In 1952, the elusive Mann joined rookie receiver Billy Howton to provide the Packers with one of the most feared receiving tandems in professional football. With a more balanced attack, Mann's receiving numbers dropped to 30 catches, but the team was more successful, finishing a respectable 6-6.

During the 1953 season, Mann was injured, missed two games and was limited in two others. He finished the season with 23 catches, but Mann's three-year total of 103 receptions was second only to Hutson for a similar period of time in Packer history, until that time.

Unfortunately, his career was cut short when he suffered a serious knee injury in the 1954 pre-season, forcing him into premature retirement at age 30. The personification of soft-spoken dignity, Mann didn't consider himself a history-maker.

"I didn't feel like I was a pioneer," Mann said prior to his Packer Hall of Fame induction in 1988. "Times change, necessities change. People become accustomed to those things (Blacks in a predominately White community)...I just hoped that my actions were such that they didn't deter future Black players from going to Green Bay. Black players were going to be more and more involved in football. I just tried to be me."

After his Packer retirement, Mann went back to Detroit, continued his education, and became a successful lawyer. He owned his own law firm for over 30 years and was still handling some cases in the 1980's.

Bob Mann made his mark with the Packers in more ways than one. On the field, he proved he was one of the best. Off the field, his exemplary conduct paved the way for future Blacks with the Packers.

Tobin Rote

When courage didn't result in team success

Never has a courageous player given so much of himself for Packer teams that got such poor results.

The best running quarterback in the history of the Packers, and the NFL, was a big Texan, Tobin Rote. The 6'2", 210-pound Rote ran better, and more often, than any other Packer, back in the early 1950's. He had speed, power and elusiveness. In addition, he was as tough as they come.

Rote led the team in passing in each of his seven seasons with the Packers. He also led the team in rushing for three seasons, and tied for second in team rushing for two more seasons. The team, however, never had a winning season while Rote was there, from 1950 through 1956, posting a 28-55-1 record, finishing last or next-to-last, five of his seven seasons.

But win or lose, Tobin Rote was most of the Packers' offense during that seven-year period. He was fiercely competitive and as tough as they come – or at least as NFL quarterbacks come. He played with a broken nose, busted ribs, broken fingers, minor concussions, sprains, cuts and other injuries that would have kept most QBs out of action. He was an NFL player who was a throwback to the 1920's and 1930's.

Bart Starr, rookie in Rote's last year with the Packers,

was amazed with his toughness. "Tobin was a very tough guy. He would be flattened time and again and keep getting up," Starr told author Tex Maule. "He took some shots that would have put most QBs out of action but he came right back and acted as though nothing had happened," Starr said.

A second-round draft choice from Rice in 1950, Rote would become a threat to run, as well as to throw a pass, every time he touched the ball. He led the Packers in rushing in 1951 with 523 yards in 76 attempts for a league-leading average gain of 6.9 per carry.

When Gene Ronzani replaced Curley Lambeau as the Packers' coach in 1950, he revised the offense and opened it up for more scoring. Ronzani's teams always caught the eyes of the fans because they played interesting offensive football. Ronzani had been a quarterback with the Bears during the days of the development of the T-system offense, and his coaching reflected that experience. He was one of the first to use the wide spread which had become increasingly popular. In his four seasons as coach, the Packers began to rebuild their reputation as crowd pleasers.

At the center of Ronzani's crowd-pleasing offensive game plan was the ruggedly handsome Rote. Ronzani wanted a quarterback who could run, as well as pass. Rote, Green Bay Packer quarterback for seven years, from 1950 to 1956, seemed to enjoy every step of the run.

Rote was a good, tough ball carrier. He had learned the trade as a fullback in high school. He still ranks among the NFL's all-time leading ground gainers and is the only quarterback on the list.

In ten seasons in the NFL, seven with Green Bay and three with Detroit, Rote amassed the following ground-gaining statistics: 601 carries, an average of 60 per season; 3,178 yards, an average of 318 per season; and an outstanding average gain of 5.1 yards per carry.

But ground gaining was only Rote's secondary contribution to the Packers. He was a quarterback, and therefore, the team's passer in a pass-conscious game. In ten NFL seasons,

PROFILES OF COURAGE • TOBIN ROTE

Tobin Rote in his rookie year in 1950. He sits next to his backup, Paul Christman at Old City Stadium in Green Bay.
Packer Hall of Fame photo

his passes gained 15,144 yards. In 1952, he lost the league's top passing honor in the final game to Norm Van Brocklin of the Los Angeles Rams. Van Brocklin wound up with an 8.47-yard average gain per pass; Rote with 8.08.

Evans Kirkby, sports writer for the *Milwaukee Journal* once wrote, "While many pro quarterbacks drop into the pocket and fire, hitting or missing with about the excitement of the clerk sorting mail, there was an electrifying suspense when Rote got the ball from center. Would he throw? Would the pass be long or short? Or would he run? If so, how far? He had runs of 55, 49 and 39 yards in his NFL career. Would he score? He scored 35 touchdowns in 10 NFL seasons."

When the yards were hard to get, as the Packers approached the opponent's goal, Rote was a powerful threat or a quarterback sneak, using the goal post as an 11th blocker and throwing his powerful body against the huge defensive linemen.

Sid Luckman, the quarterback coach for the Chicago Bears, once said, "Whenever you play Green Bay, you've just got to hope Rote won't have a hot day. If he does, he'll kill you,"

In 1954, Rote set a league record by throwing 382 passes and had the highest number completed in the season, 180. In 1956, Rote threw more passes than any other NFL quarterback (308), completed more (146), gained more yards (2,203), and scored more touchdowns (18).

Rote's seven-year career with the Packers was up and down. Often wild and inconsistent with his passes when he first joined the Packers, the team kept looking for a more consistent passer at the quarterback position.

Rote, taken by the Packers in the second round of the 1950 draft, suffered through a tough rookie season, throwing a league-high 24 interceptions. Facing a challenge from a talented passer named Bobby Thomason in 1951, he improved his passing stats and really came on as a runner with his team, leading total yards rushing.

Still looking for a pure passer, the Packers took Babe Parilli with their first choice in 1952, and Rote faced another battle for the quarterback job. He responded with one of best passing performances of his career, while sharing time with the new challenger.

In fact, the current NFL passer rating system would rank this as Rote's best season. But a year later, he reverted to the level of his rookie year, and the only thing that saved him from being benched was the fact that Parilli, who again shared the job with him, was no better.

When the military drafted Parilli before the 1954 season, Rote took over once again as the Packers' full-time quarterback. For the next three years, he starred for a series of mediocre Green Bay teams, leading the NFL twice in attempts, completions and touchdown passes, and once in passing yards. His best year was 1956, when he led the league in all those categories and also ran for eleven touchdowns.

In 1957, the Packers traded Rote to Detroit, where he figured to serve as a backup to Bobby Layne. But Layne broke his leg during the season, and for the first time, the veteran Rote found himself leading a team with a chance for the title. The Lions tied the 49ers for the western title, and fell behind 27-7 in the divisional playoff game before coming back to win 31-27. Rote completed 16 of 30 passes, for 214 yards and a touchdown, while directing one of the NFL's greatest comebacks.

After his NFL tour, Rote went on to play three years in the Canadian league where he twice tied the league record by throwing seven touchdown passes in a single game, leading Toronto to championships in 1960 and 1961.

Subsequently, he spent two seasons with San Diego in the American Football League. He was the league's leading passer with a 14.76-yard average on 286 passes, and the league's 'Most Valuable Player' in 1963 as San Diego won the championship. In 1964, Rote again led San Diego to a division championship but the Chargers lost in the title playoff to Buffalo.

As a Packer, Rote could be very good when he was good and very bad when he had an off day. Lisle Blackbourn,

PROFILES OF COURAGE • TOBIN ROTE

Rote led the Packers in passing in every one of his seven seasons and led the team in rushing in three seasons. *Milwaukee Journal photo*

PROFILES OF COURAGE • TOBIN ROTE

Rote was a strong passer, but not always on target. His coach, Lisle Blackbourn said, "When Tobin is hot, he's one of the best. When he's cold, well..."

Rote was traded to Detroit after the 1956 season. Never has a courageous player given so much of himself for Packer teams that got such poor results.   *Packer Hall of Fame photos*

Rote's coach at Green Bay for four years, one said, "When Tobin is hot, he is positively the greatest of them all. And when he is cold, well…"

But Blackbourn also once described Rote as, "…the greatest competitor I ever saw." It was a characteristic, perhaps, that made Rote such an exciting player to watch and contributed to his induction to the Packer Hall of Fame in 1974.

After retiring from football and starting his own company in the Detroit area, he, his wife and four children lived in suburban Birmingham, Michigan. Rote died at the age of 72 on June 27, 2000, in a Saginaw, Michigan, hospital after suffering a heart attack nearly two weeks after undergoing back surgery. But Packer fans of the 1950's will never forget the best, and one of the toughest running quarterbacks in Green Bay's long history in the NFL.

Bart Starr

Perseverance in overcoming prolonged adversity

The piercing shoulder pain returned, and along with it, the unbearable realization that his 15-year career as the Packers' quarterback may be over. His 36-year-old body now felt much older. He had missed so many games in the last four seasons with the torn up shoulder, torn biceps, separated elbow, and broken ribs.

Now, as a last resort, he would have surgery on the aching shoulder that he had suffered with for four seasons. Rest, exhausting exercises, and medication for five months hadn't worked. The pain was back. He couldn't throw a ball 15 yards. Truth was, he could hardly grip the ball.

The surgery was performed at the Mayo Clinic. The prognosis looked good. He returned to his home in Green Bay to heal and get ready for the 1971 season – his 16th. Three days later he almost bled to death.

His wife, Cherry, noticed how pale he looked – like 'death warmed over.' He told her he felt very weak. She checked the bandage covering the surgically repaired shoulder. It was covered in blood. She rushed to the phone and called the Packers' team physician to come over quickly. The doctor told them both, it was a good thing Cherry had called right away. Had she waited another 24 hours, it may have been too late.

After a return to Mayo for the repair, he was laid up for weeks and could not return to practice until near the end of the season. There had been some nerve damage as a result of the operation, causing him problems in gripping the ball. He wore a thin leather glove in an attempt to improve his grip, but it didn't help. He could no longer throw effectively.

His final appearance as a Packer came in the last game of the 1971 season. He could no longer throw with any consistency and even asked Coach Dan Devine to take him out in the third quarter when it became obvious he couldn't even hit receivers who were wide open. The coach said, "No," to his request, and the Packers lost, 27-6

It was finally over, after 16 seasons. The old quarterback tried to come back for another season in 1972, but he realized a couple of weeks into training camp that his body would no longer allow him to play anywhere near the level of previous years, when he simply had been the best there ever was.

Between 1960 and 1967, Bart Starr led the Packers to six NFL Championship games, losing only once to the Philadelphia Eagles in 1960. While contemporaries like Johnny Unitas, Frank Ryan, Y.A. Tittle and John Brodie received more attention, Starr consistently won big games and piled up championships. His poise and leadership earned him 'Most Valuable Player' status in both Super Bowls I and II.

Starr led the league in passing in 1962, 1964 and 1966, and was named to the Pro Bowl four times. Until Brett Favre came along, he had held the Packer career record for most seasons as a player, 16. He is in both the Pro Football and Packer Halls of Fame. In 2008, Starr was named best quarterback in the National Football League, of all time.

He is the epitome of toughness and courage. He humbly credits *attitude* for those noble characteristics. He once said, long after his playing days, "Enthusiasm. Toughness. Courage. They are all derivatives of *attitude*. It's what enables you to handle the burden. You know what's expected of you, and you come to the point where you welcome it, where you embrace it."

Embrace the 'burden' he did. Starr's *attitude* carried him through six years of disappointing and inglorious football. Most young men would have tossed in the towel somewhere along those six years of frustration and moved on with their lives. But Starr didn't quit, and his *attitude* kept him playing long after his body could deliver the play of those brilliant years, because he didn't want to quit on the new coach, and the young player, Don Horn, who was set to replace him, wasn't ready yet. So he kept on playing when he could easily have retired at the top of his game.

It wasn't because he wanted to beef up his already remarkable stats that he kept playing, but to help new head Coach Phil Bengtson, who was replacing the legendary Vince Lombardi, and to guide a young man expected to fill his shoes. It is a tribute to Starr, whose perseverance in overcoming prolonged adversity is well documented.

In light of this, you would never believe Bart Starr, the most winning quarterback in Packer history, once suffered from a serious lack of self-confidence. It all started when Starr went from being a high school All-American with a promising college career and the potential to be the best passer in the University of Alabama history, to riding the bench his junior and senior year.

The pros thought so little of Starr's potential, he slid all the way to 17th pick (by the Packers), the 200th college player selected in 1956. He spent the next four years as a some-time starter, but mostly backup quarterback, with a fractured, continually sinking confidence level, kept afloat only by a stronger, more determined will.

Then, in 1959, Starr's disciplined will connected with the iron will of a new Packer coach, Vince Lombardi. Starr's confidence climbed to amazing heights over the next few years, and his life changed forever.

But between his junior year in college and the first four, grim years with the Packers, Starr overcame confidence-crushing experiences and adversity that would have sent most football players packing. However, Starr's extraordinary perseverance and will to succeed prevailed.

Until today, he has probably been the most popular retired Packer to have ever played in Green Bay, a living legend to Packer fans everywhere. Now that Brett Favre has retired, he will move into that role.

There was a time, early in his career with the Packers, that it looked like Starr was destined to become just another washed up pro quarterback. However, with a new, tough-minded coach, plus his own tenacity and perseverance, Starr wrote a much different ending to his pro football story.

Starr was born in Montgomery, Alabama, in 1935. His father, Ben, a master sergeant in the United States Air Force during most of Bart's teen years, encouraged him to play football. Bart, too small to be much of a player in junior high school and freshman year in high school, almost quit football.

His father, a tough disciplinarian, put Bart into hard labor after school, helping him decide to stick it out in football. By the time he was a junior, Starr became the starting quarterback at Sidney Lanier High School. After a standout senior year, Starr was named to the high school All-American team. That was followed by a football scholarship to the University of Alabama.

In his freshman year, Starr was the backup to the senior quarterback as Alabama went to the Orange Bowl. He took over the starter position his sophomore year and led the team to the Cotton Bowl. He had developed a command presence on the field. He was inspiring confidence and respect from his teammates.

It was at this time that Starr's promising football fortunes hit adversity. He hurt his back during his junior year and missed most of the games. The team did not do well and his head coach left Alabama.

His senior year brought more disappointment. The new coach put in a different offensive system and named a younger quarterback to start. Starr spent most of the season

PROFILES OF COURAGE • BART STARR

In the summer of 1956, Bart's father helped him prepare for his pro tryout with the Packers.

Photo from "Bart Starr" by Tex Maule

on the bench. The new system didn't work. Alabama went winless, going 0-10.

Looking back, Starr said he had been devastated, "I was psychologically demoralized. My senior year was a disaster." His wife, Cherry, whom he had married during his junior year, was his strongest supporter, trying to keep his spirits up.

Since he played sporadically in his last two years at Alabama, Starr was not a hot prospect for the pros. He ended up drafted in the 17th, and last, round of the college draft of 1956. That summer, he spent most of his time throwing footballs through a tire that hung by a rope at his in-laws' house.

When Starr reported to Coach Liz Blackbourn at the Packers pre-season training camp at Stevens Point State College, he was one of five quarterbacks trying to make the team. Six-year veteran Tobin Rote was the starter, so the best Starr hoped for was a backup spot.

Rote befriended Starr early in the camp and gave him tips to help his progress. At one point, Rote told Starr to strengthen his throwing arm, "Your arm is not strong enough for the pros, you need more zip."

Rote's wisdom was fed by his hunger to play, even in the pre-season. There were plays in which the sturdy leader was flattened – knocked out by a blindside shot – only to re-enter the huddle on the next play. "Tobin was a very tough guy," Starr told football writer Tex Maule. "He had his own style, which wasn't at all like mine, and he was set in it. But he was thoughtful and helpful with me and gave me some very useful tips."

Starr played in some of the exhibition games and impressed Coach Blackbourn enough with his work ethic to make the team. Blackbourn noticed Starr watched more game film and studied the playbook more than any other rookie. After he made the final cuts, Starr recalled, "It was one of the happiest days of my life."

Starr played little in 1956, throwing only 44 passes, completing 24 with two touchdowns and three interceptions.

The team finished a disappointing 4-8.

After the 1956 season, Starr was called to active duty in the Air Force, based on his ROTC commission. However, his service time was short because he flunked the physical due to a back problem. When he was given a military medical discharge, in the summer of 1957, he and Cherry moved into an apartment in Green Bay.

Rote was traded to the Lions before the 1957 season, but the Packers brought back Vito 'Babe' Parilli to start at quarterback. Parilli, a standout at Kentucky, had been the Packers' first draft choice in 1952, before he was drafted into the service, and then traded to the Browns. Obtained in a trade with the Browns, Parilli wasn't the same quarterback he had been, so Starr saw a considerable amount of playing time during the 1957 season.

Parilli led the Packers to victory over the Bears in the 1957 opener in the new City Stadium, which was later renamed Lambeau Field. Then the team went into a losing streak. Starr took over as starter and put up decent numbers for the season. He led the team with 215 attempts, 117 completions (for 54%), and eight touchdowns, but he also had ten interceptions.

In 1957, the Packers finished last with a 3-9 record, causing Blackbourn to be fired as coach. Long-time popular Packer assistant coach, Ray 'Scooter' McLean, replaced him. McLean couldn't settle on a starting quarterback for the entire 1958 season. As a result, Parilli and Starr split playing time almost equally, both having 157 attempts. Starr completed more passes, 78 to 68, but Parilli had more yardage gained and touchdown passes, 10-3. Starr ended the season with a poor 41 Q.B. rating, which suffered primarily because of his team high thirteen interceptions.

After three years with the Packers, Bart Starr looked like just another average NFL quarterback who would perhaps play with several pro teams before drifting into football obscurity. They said he was an inconsistent passer and lacked the leadership skills needed to be a successful pro quarterback. At the end of the 1958 season, his third with the

Packers, Starr was relegated to third string. His confidence was shot and his future in the NFL looked doubtful.

Starr was the starter early in the 1958 season, but his only impressive game was against the Lions, in the second game. He was 19 for 31, for 196 yards and one touchdown in a 13-13 tie with Detroit, the 1957 first place team in the Western Conference and World Champions. Parilli replaced him as starter by game five against the Eagles and the Packers won, 38-35. It was to be the their only win all season. They lost the next week to the Colts, 56-0, giving Starr another chance to start the following Sunday against the Bears at Wrigley Field.

By this point in the season, the offensive line had just about caved in. As a result, Starr was rushed and hammered on almost every play and took a terrible physical beating. In a game against the Chicago Bears, he was thrown for 50 yards in losses, attempting to pass. On one play, he was tossed for a loss, fumbled and the Bears recovered for a touchdown in a 24-10 Chicago victory. It was not a pretty sight.

With his in-and-out status as the Packer quarterback, Starr's confidence sagged. In a late November issue of the *Milwaukee Journal*, sports reporter Chuck Johnson analyzed the team's quarterbacks. Of the 24-year-old Starr, he said, "According to the Packers' coaches and teammates, Starr has the potential to be a great quarterback. He has the smarts, the 'voice', the arm, and can run well enough. However, Starr lacks two things – experience, and confidence in his own ability."

One teammate said Starr was, "…not tough enough – he was too 'nice' in the huddle and doesn't fire up the guys. He sets up plays well and is good on hand-offs; he just needs to have more meanness or cockiness."

By now Starr was physically beaten up due to the Packers' porous line, and his self-confidence was at a low point. McLean had lost confidence in Starr, as well. He relegated the battered quarterback to third string. Starr played very little in the remaining six games of the worst season in

PROFILES OF COURAGE • BART STARR

Early in his fourth year with the Packers, Starr still did not get high grades from the coaches.
Photo from Tom Pigeon Collection

Starr took over the number one quarterback spot in mid-1960 season and went to become one of the best in spite of prolonged adversity.

Bart Starr and Vince Lombardi before a College All-Star game in Chicago.
AP Wire photo

Packer history. They would finish 1-10-1. Scooter quit at the end of the season to avoid being fired, and to become an assistant coach with the Lions.

However, Starr was not about to quit after the disastrous season. "It was miserable, sickening, disappointing, testing," Starr told author David Maraniss. Starr added, "I did not even consider quitting."

Vince Lombardi became the new coach in 1959 and Starr's life was about to make a drastic turnabout. But not right away. In the beginning, Lombardi was not impressed with Starr. "I looked at the movies of the club and decided that the first thing I needed to win was help at quarterback," he said later, "I didn't think Starr or Parilli could do the job, so I traded for Lamar McHan."

"That was a real shock," Starr said. "I wasn't happy at all when Mr. Lombardi traded for another quarterback. I had been in the league for three years and it looked like I might be number two quarterback for the rest of my life. But I never even considered quitting. It was another challenge."

"I was impressed with Lombardi the first time I met him, even if he wasn't that impressed with me," Starr said. "I didn't blame him for bringing in a new quarterback, but I decided to show him that I could do the job."

Starr remained the number two quarterback for Lombardi until late in the 1959 season. Then he started the last four games – all victories – and the Packers finished 7-5. It was the Packers' first winning season in twelve years.

Starr was beginning to change the coachs' impression of his abilities. After eight games of that season, Lombardi asked four assistants to evaluate each player on the roster. What were the player's strengths? What were his weaknesses? What was his potential? Would he be an asset or a detriment to the rebuilding process? Should he be protected or left unprotected for the expansion draft following the 1959 season that would stock the new Dallas Cowboys?

These amazing evaluations have only recently come to light outside the Packers' offices. They were discovered in stacks of football-related material left by the late Phil

Bengtson, who had been Lombardi's chief assistant. It was Bengtson's son, Jay, who published a book in 2001, releasing the evaluations.

Bengtson, who also succeeded Lombardi as head coach and eventually became general manager, died in 1994. The other assistants who participated in these evaluations were Norb Hecker, Bill Austin, and John 'Red' Cochran.

The appraisals were offered after the eighth game of the 12-game season. The Packers had surprised everyone by winning their first three games, but then fell into a five-game losing streak. Starr, of whom one coach said, "I do not believe we can win with Starr," took over the starting quarterback role and led the team to four straight wins.

Here are their evaluations of Starr – not exactly glowing testimonials.

"Bart is a fair thrower – not at all consistent. He is a very smart boy but lacks leadership, which we must have. When he is in the game, he does a fair job but never seems to get us in for the big scores. His past history is about the same. He is, as I'd put it, a good second string QB. Could be better next year, but I doubt it."

"Not a consistent passer. Not a take-charge type of player. I do not believe we can win with Starr."

"A number two quarterback at best, but smart and serious enough to do a satisfactory job in this capacity."

"A capable fill-in at best. He should be kept until we get a better boy with promise to be worked with, rather than have Starr take up our time."

Starr reported to the team in the pre-season of 1960 thinking he would finally be the number one quarterback. Assistant coach Red Cochran, the backfield coach, thought he could be.

In his little coach's notebook that I obtained after Red's death, Cochran wrote, "Starr was smart, had improved leadership and was excellent at short passes." He noted, Starr's weak points were his "…long passes and lack of confidence." However, Red also wrote, "Starr has great desire, mental toughness and his confidence is improving."

PROFILES OF COURAGE • BART STARR

Starr was injured in 1970 and was never able to come back to the same level of play that had been his trademark for years.

By the early '70s Starr was starting to feel the wear of numerous injuries.

Milwaukee Journal photo

PROFILES OF COURAGE • BART STARR

Bart Starr calls for quiet as Packers advance Rams in Green Bay on his "day," in 1970.

Between halves of the Ram game, an emotional Bart Starr is congratulated by Stars of 1962. Among them (left to right) Paul Hornung, Max McGee and Bob Skoronski. Starr got a standing ovation that lasted over one minute.

Milwaukee Journal photo

Starr did start the first game of the 1960 season, but was pulled. McHan finished in a 17-14 loss to the Bears. McHan started the next four games – all victories. But McHan struggled in the sixth game and Starr came in to lead the team to a 19-13 win over the Steelers. Starr would be the starting quarterback from then on, until near the end of his career, when injuries cut into his ability to perform.

In the twilight of his famed career, the Packers held a special day for Starr. The ceremonies took place at Lambeau Field in a game against the Rams in 1970. There was a heartwarming standing ovation when Starr trotted through the goal posts as his name was introduced. In fact, public address announcer Gary Knafelc was able to say only, "And at quarterback...," before the roar drowned him out.

The halftime ceremony was a special time, with the members of the 1962 Packer team also trotting through the goalposts and being greeted by deafening applause. Western Union displayed a telegram with 40,000 names, all expressing thanks to Starr for his contributions to Packer fans everywhere. The telegrams, if placed side-by-side, would stretch across five football fields. A bag of letters was carried onto the field. It contained 3,200 individual letters addressed to Starr, again, each one in its own way saying a big, "Thank you, Bart!"

The throng in Lambeau rose and applauded for nearly a minute when Starr came onto the field. "These 15 years in Green Bay," Starr said, his voice breaking, "have been the most memorable ones that a man could ever want. I feel like the luckiest person on earth."

When the shoulder injury ended his playing career before the 1972 season, Starr became an assistant coach under Dan Devine and helped the Packers win the Central Division championship that season. In 1975, Starr was named head coach and general manager of the Packers. He posted a poor 52-76-3 record over the next nine seasons. While his outstanding playing career turned out to be one Packer fans will long remember, his coaching tenure with the Packers would be very forgettable. It turned out to be a sad finish for a dedicated Packer who is in the Pro Football Hall of Fame and Packer Hall of Fame.

Early on the Monday following the end of the 1983 season, Packer board president Judge Parins walked into Starr's office at Lambeau Field. "I want to talk to you, Bart," Parins said entering Starr's office. Starr replied that his assistant coaches were waiting for him and asked Parins if was going to take long. "Not long at all. You don't have to worry about your meeting, because as of this moment I am relieving you of your coaching position," Parins said coldly and without emotion, according to Starr's autobiography.

Parins left Starr's office without another word. He didn't thank Starr for his efforts, his 26-year contribution to the team – or even show any regret about having to make the decision.

Starr closed the door, sat at his desk and wept.

Still, he would later say, "I have a very strong attachment for this team and the Packers organization. I feel it's the greatest organization in pro sports… its tradition, heritage, record and image. I've felt very privileged to have been able to play my entire career with Green Bay."

Regardless of his ignominious departure, Starr is one of the most popular and respected of all retired Packers. His amazing accomplishments, determined will, courage, and self-discipline as a player in overcoming prolonged adversity are legendary.

Jerry Kramer

Uncommon comeback from life-threatening accidents, nothing short of miraculous

Jerry Kramer never should have been able to play football for his small town Idaho high school, let alone college or pro ball. Two major accidents affecting his physical ability when he was teenager should have ended his aspirations of ever playing football – at any level – *especially* professional. But he did. It was nothing short of miraculous.

A hunting accident at age 16, with a double-barrelled shotgun, nearly blew away his right arm, to the point the doctor was going to amputate. A year later, in a freak accident, a cluster of splinters from a board he stepped on, stabbed up through his groin and lodged there.

They managed to pull out some of the wooden daggers, but it took major surgery to get out another seven-inch long splinter that had lodged in his back. The doctors told him that one of the splinters had been just about to puncture his spine.

After both of these disastrous events of bad luck, Kramer's doctor told him to forget any idea of playing football. Kramer, known for his fearlessness and stubborn determination, regained most of the use of his arm and shook off the piercingly painful splinters that had accidentally entered his groin, back and stomach.

He did go on to play football, well enough at his high school in Sand Point, Idaho, to get a chance to become a pretty good offensive and defensive lineman at the University of Idaho. It was good enough to get Kramer drafted by the Packers in the fourth round in 1958.

Kramer went from a fairly decent football player to becoming one of the best guards in the NFL during his playing career in Green Bay. Vince Lombardi once said, "Jerry Kramer is the best guard in the league – some say in the *history* of the game."

Kramer was the starting right guard when Green Bay won five NFL championships between 1961-67. He was named to three Pro Bowls, was named All-Pro six times and was inducted into the Packers Hall of Fame in 1975. He was also Green Bay's place-kicker in 1962-63 and his book, Instant Replay, is one of the best-selling sports books of all time. Kramer was named to the all-NFL First 50 Years Team, and his block on Dallas' Jethro Pugh sprung Bart Starr for a game-winning touchdown in the 'Ice Bowl,' the most famous football game ever played.

However, overcoming two unnerving accidents that nearly cost him his life might be the real Jerry Kramer story. The first occurred at the age of 16 when he decided to go hunting with his grandfather's shotgun one November day. In attempting to get to his feet after resting on a large boulder, he slammed the cocked hammers of the shotgun against the rock. The resultant blast virtually shattered his right arm, leaving ligaments and muscle hanging out, and about 17 pellets pierced his side.

He was rushed to a hospital and was listed in critical condition for seven days. "I remember the doctor coming into the room with my parents and I was in kind of a fog yet. The doctor took a pen out of his breast pocket and sort of drew it around my elbow to show my folks where he was going to amputate," Kramer recalled.

But with the usual Kramer fortune that seems to follow misfortune, the arm took a turn for the better with the help of some skin grafting, to allow Kramer to regain the full use

PROFILES OF COURAGE • JERRY KRAMER

Left: Kramer shows the splinters of wood removed from his body, 12 years apart, that nearly cost him his life.
Packer Hall of Fame photo

Right: Kramer overcame injuries as a teen that should have kept him from becoming one of the NFL's best guards in the 1960s – but they didn't!

Kramer blocks for Jim Grabowski against the Bears at Wrigley Field. It was his last game in 1968.
Chicago Tribune photo

of his arm. A year later, another accident would cause him serious health problem for years to come. The accident happened in Sand Point when Jerry came home from swimming and found a calf running loose on the family acres. He spent a half hour chasing the animal before his father arrived, and together, they cornered it.

"I was just grabbing for the calf's tail," Kramer relates, "when I stepped hard on an old board, a one-by-six about ten feet long. The board snapped into two pieces and one end of it sprung in the air and caught me right in the groin.

"I laid down and pulled it out while Dad called the doctor, but the doctor misunderstood and thought we were coming in to see him. I laid there about an hour before the doctor finally came and took me to the hospital.

"They probed around and couldn't find any more splinters, but the next day, I started getting a pain in my back. At first, nobody paid attention to it, but after a couple of days, the doctor actually went out to our house and tried to fit the board back together. He discovered there was still a big piece missing.

"I was rushed 70 miles to the hospital in Spokane, and there they found another piece of wood, about 3/4" wide and 7-1/2" long, lodged way up in my back just about to puncture the spine."

They thought they had gotten all the splinters the first time, but 12 years later, would discover they hadn't. In the meantime, Kramer would suffer two more injuries, either of which could have cut his Packer career short.

The first took place late in the Packers' 1960 season. While watching game film in preparation for the last game of the season, Kramer noticed he was having trouble seeing out of his left eye. An examination that week showed he had a detached retina.

The doctors told him if he played any more football that season, a blow to the head could cost him his eyesight in that eye. He took the risk because the Packers were about to play the Philadelphia Eagles for the NFL Championship.

After the game, which the Packers lost to the Eagles, he

PROFILES OF COURAGE • JERRY KRAMER

Jerry Kramer – a Packer profile of true grit.

Packer Hall of Fame photo

had a new surgical procedure performed at the University of Wisconsin Hospital. It was a success and his eyesight was saved.

The second nearly-career-ending injury took place in the sixth game of the Packers' 1961 season. Playing the Vikings in Minneapolis, Kramer got hammered on the opening kick-off. He was carried off on a stretcher in severe pain. He found out, after the game, that he had broken his left ankle in two places, in addition to severely stretching ligaments. His season was over. To mend the shattered bones in his ankle, the doctors put in a steel pin the size of a stove bolt and told him to forget football. Once again, Kramer ignored their advice.

In the off-season, he lifted weights, and walked and ran to strengthen the ankle and leg. By early in the 1962 season, Kramer was back in the starting lineup. He wondered if the worst was behind him. It wasn't.

By the middle of the 1964 season, he began to get terribly sick. A series of operations failed to clear up a mysterious internal ailment in his large intestine. He ended up having eight operations. The first one took out a tumor, about to burst and the size of a grapefruit. Had it burst, it would have killed him. He finally ended up at the Mayo Clinic in Rochester, Minnesota.

He was losing weight. His temperature had risen well over 100 degrees; his large intestine had burst and he was sick all over. He thought he was going to die. The doctors performed an emergency colostomy. In addition to still feeling sick, he now felt humiliated, the wound, still draining, making a foul mess.

Still in the hospital, his weight continued to drop; he couldn't sit, felt sick all the time and was depressed. Then he developed pneumonia. The nightmare had started. At times he couldn't control his weeping. "I was sick, so sick, so damn sick. I was a mess, my wound draining, my intestine hanging out; my weight was down from 255 pounds to fewer than 200. I had absolutely no control. I was standing up, and the stool poured out and started trickling down my leg and onto my feet and between my toes, and I couldn't stand it. I was so helpless, so humiliated, I had considered going out a window," Kramer recalled.

He didn't jump. He cried. He felt sorry for himself. He even called his parents and old friends from the hospital to kind of say, "Good-bye."

He would relate later in his book, *Farewell to Football*, "I didn't jump. I cried. I felt so sorry for myself. Dan Currie, one of my teammates, phoned me, and I couldn't talk to him. I choked up. I couldn't hold back the tears. I started thinking about my kids, thinking I'd never see them again. I watched 'The Rifleman' on television, and I saw a scene with Chuck Connors and the little boy who always accompanied him, and I began crying again. I started making phone calls. I called my mother and my father, my brother, my closest friends from high school and college, all the people who'd meant a lot to me over the years. I didn't actually say good-bye to them, but I felt I was saying good-bye. I was twenty-eight years old, and I was ready to go."

"My weight kept sinking. I couldn't eat. It went down to 203 pounds, the lightest I'd been since high school. I was filled with nothing but self-pity." Kramer said.

And then, for some reason, his mind wandered back to all the sick children he had met during his many trips to hospitals. Kramer said, "I looked back and I told myself, 'you've had a great life. You've gone more places and have done more things than eighty or ninety percent of the people in the world. You've had it pretty good. You've got no complaints.' I made peace with myself."

Kramer finally got better and left the hospital, but still had the colostomy. He related, "The damned colostomy was an ever-present thing. It was like a grotesque growth that clung to me."

Months later, with his wound still not healing properly, they operated again. The operation lasted six-and-a-half hours.

Lo and behold, at last they discovered the cause of the illness he had been suffering from for the past year.

Unbelievably, four more slivers of wood were found stuck in his intestine, left over from his accident twelve years prior. Finally it was over. Ten days later, he was playing golf.

Kramer, now living in Boise, Idaho, ended his outstanding career with the Packers after the 1968 season. He went into the commercial driving business, and then built apartments with former Packer Don Chandler. He started a film company in Los Angeles and dabbled in the restaurant business. He worked with oil and gas exploration, coal mining, telecommunications and nutrition. Kramer has also been a consultant for a security company and a hospital group.

Two years ago, he released a CD that he produced from tape recordings left over from materials he had gathered for the book he wrote in the late 1960's, titled *Instant Replay*.

He is presently involved with several other former Packers and NFL stars of the past to raise funds for the less fortunate former NFL players. The money raised is placed in the Gridiron Greats Fund, a charitable trust, "…that will help former players pay their medical bills and supplement meager pensions," Kramer said.

Kramer knows all about hard times and medical bills. Now he feels it's time to help other fellow players who can't help themselves.

Ray Nitschke

The courage to overcome self-destruction to become the best linebacker in Packer history

Lombardi called him, "...the spearhead of our defense." Indeed, he was. A pillar on one end of the NFL's best defenses through most of the 1960's, Ray Nitschke was simply the best linebacker in Packer history.

A ferocious 6'-3", 235-pound middle linebacker, Nitschke was the heart of the Green Bay defense. He epitomized the hard hitting tenacity and cool professionalism of the Packers during the dynasty years. In 1969, one sportswriter panel recognized Ray's rare performances by naming him "...the best linebacker in the NFL's first 50 years."

He was named to the NFL's 50th Anniversary Team in 1994. In 1978, he was presented the top recognition a professional football player can receive when he was inducted into the prestigious Pro Football Hall of Fame. He was also inducted into the Packer Hall of Fame the same year.

These were all honors Nitschke richly deserved as a result of his outstanding play in fifteen years as a Green Bay Packer.

However, the honors and the majority of the fifteen years almost never happened. Nitschke had been hell-bent on acting out a self-destructive behavior that could easily have cut his Packer career shorter, probably ten years shorter.

If it hadn't been for one or two people in Nitschke's life, he could have ended up just another drunken bum who would spend his remaining days bragging about his days as a football player to anyone who would listen.

Instead, it did indeed, turn out somewhat different.

To begin with, Nitschke had had a rather disastrous childhood, which no doubt contributed to his self-destructive behavior. His father had died in a freak car accident when Ray was three, and his mother had died of a sudden illness when he was just thirteen.

It fell to his older brother to raise him in a Chicago suburb as best he could. For the most part, Nitschke was left to fend for himself. As a result, he became a rough-and-tumble teen who often fought other kids while roaming the streets.

He carried his tough-guy attitude to the University of Illinois where he was constantly in and out of trouble. Being a valuable member of the football team kept him from getting kicked out of school, but it only fueled his aggressive behavior on and off the field.

In 1958, the Packers drafted Nitschke in the third round. He brought his loud, obnoxious, brawling behavior to Green Bay. When he wasn't playing and practicing, he lived in the bars and looked for fights, which he found, more often than not. While he showed the coaches raw talent and wild-man aggressiveness on the field, he barely made the team in 1958.

"I didn't have anybody to love, or to love me," recalled Nitschke. "I took it out on the guys carrying the ball on the field." His teammate, Jerry Kramer, wrote in his book, *Distant Replay*, "We had a few disagreements during our early years in Green Bay. The last one, I remember well. We were out partying, drinking more than we should have, and Ray said some things he shouldn't have said. One thing led to another, and finally he asked if I wanted to step outside. I said, 'Hell, yes,' and started for the door. I looked over my shoulder and Ray was right behind me. I said to myself, 'Oh, Self, you are in trouble!' I figured we were about to get serious and I had better get my bluff in first.

PROFILES OF COURAGE • RAY NITSCHKE

Intense, relentless, angry in pursuit and always ready to hit: Ray Nitschke was rightfully voted the best middle linebacker in the NFL's first 50 years.

"You've got to like contact," Nitschke once said. "If you're not willing to hit people you don't belong on the field." I grew up belting the other kids in the neighborhod, " he recalled. "I felt I was somebody who didn't have anything and I took it out on everybody."

Nitschke played 15 seasons for the Packers, the second longest career in team history. He was most valuable player of the 1962 championship game victory over the New York Giants.

Ray and Jackie on "Ray Nitschke Day," 1972.

Packer Hall of Fame photos

"I turned and grabbed Ray around the throat and I said I was ready to tear his head off. I backed him up against a brick wall and said I was crazy enough to fight or drink, whichever way he wanted it. He looked at me and said, 'No, man, you're my teammate, I don't want to fight you.' And we went back inside, fortunately for me."

Over the next three years, Nitschke was relegated to special teams and was an occasional spot starter. In the meantime, he sulked, fumed and got into the doghouse with Lombardi, while continuing to drink and brawl. He almost got cut several times during his first three years in Green Bay.

In 1959, one of the Packers' assistant coaches wrote, "[Nitschke] will always be in trouble and causing trouble. Seems like he will always be too at erratic defense. Should be good trade material." (from *The Glory Years – The 1959 Packers* by Len Wagner).

In short, Nitschke's time as a Packer was coming to a screeching halt. His all-out aggressive play on the field could not offset his self-destructive behavior which Lombardi could no longer tolerate.

If defensive coach Phil Bengtson had not been in his corner, Nitschke would have been gone sooner. Bengtson believed in Nitschke and often protected him from Lombardi's wrath and his practice of emotionally kicking him off the team.

Late in the 1960 season, Bengtson talked Lombardi into putting Nitschke into starting middle linebacker position. The defense was giving up too many points and the Packers were locked in a four-game race for the Western Conference title. The coaches were looking for a way to tighten up the defense. They found it in Nitschke.

It was the beginning of the turnaround in Nitschke's football life. He replaced starter Tom Bettis, who also was in Lombardi's doghouse after they had had a locker room confrontation regarding what Lombardi thought was poor play on Bettis' part.

Nitschke was taller, heavier, and faster than Bettis. It was the break Nitschke had been waiting for to prove he should be the starter.

He was beginning to win Lombardi's favor, when just before the last game against the Rams in the 1960 season, he screwed up again.

Lombardi had a strict rule that no player could drink at the bar. A surprise visit by the coach caught Nitschke drinking at the hotel bar in Los Angeles. As Lombardi walked by him, he said, "You're done – you're through, Nitschke."

Once again, Bengtson tried to persuade Lombardi not to kick Nitschke off the team. Lombardi said he wouldn't put Nitschke back on the team himself – but would put the matter to a team vote. It was 39-0 to keep Ray.

Nitschke's outstanding play in the last game against the Rams and in the championship game against the Eagles justified his teammates' confidence in him. His tough, aggressive play had finally earned him his full-time starting spot at middle linebacker. It was a big change.

Another event, and one person in particular, would complete Nitschke's changed life off the field forever. That one person was an attractive, dark-haired Green Bay waitress by the name of Jackie Forchette. For Ray, it was love at first sight. For Jackie, it took a little longer. Nitschke's wild, drinking, fighting reputation was no secret in Green Bay.

She said no to his first few requests for a date, but he was persistent. She finally gave in to shut him up. But as she got to know Ray better, she could see a different side of this giant of a man – a gentler, kinder, loving side he had never shown in these parts before.

They were married in the summer of 1961. He gave up drinking entirely. Cold turkey. He admitted his drinking had been a crutch to cover up his own loneliness and insecurities that went way back. Now that he had Jackie, he didn't need a crutch.

The transformation in Nitschke's life was dramatic and sudden. Jackie's loving influence transformed this football madman into a loving husband and father of their three adopted children. He continuously played with them. He had never had a childhood of his own, but it was obvious he loved them and all children.

"He probably made a greater journey to success than anybody I've ever known in my life," former Green Bay Packer teammate Bob Skoronski said. "Coming from the background that he did and the bringing up that he had, to what he was here – absolutely amazing. He was still that gruff guy to the public that knew Ray as a football player, but he also was a very loving and caring guy. You know, he found the only girl in the country who could tame him, and she did. Jackie was a great match. Don't overlook that."

Of course, his play on the field continued to improve, as well. His reputation as a tough, aggressive, 'give-em-hell,' grind-the-opponent-to-dust player grew to legendary proportions.

Nitschke has said that playing middle linebacker for the Green Bay Packers was a survival type of thing, and that if you weren't willing to hit people, you didn't belong on the field. "You want them to have respect for you when they run a play at you," he once said. "You want them to be a little shy, and a little shier next time. You want them to remember you're in there."

Any team that ever played against the Packers was well aware of Nitschke's presence. In addition to his smash-mouth football, he was downright ferocious looking. With his dark-rimmed glasses off, he continually squinted. With his teeth out, there was always that cruel looking curve to his mouth.

His uniform was often spotted with blood – his own, and his opponents' – his forearms covered with tape. There was never a meaner, tougher-looking player.

The painful phasing out of Nitschke came in 1971, when Dan Devine moved a rookie, Jim Carter, to the middle and told Nitschke to sit down. It was a dreadful experience for both Carter and Nitschke.

In the summer of 1973, Nitschke was preparing for a 16th season with the Packers, but ended up retiring later in training camp. He said, "Even though I have known that the

PROFILES OF COURAGE • RAY NITSCHKE

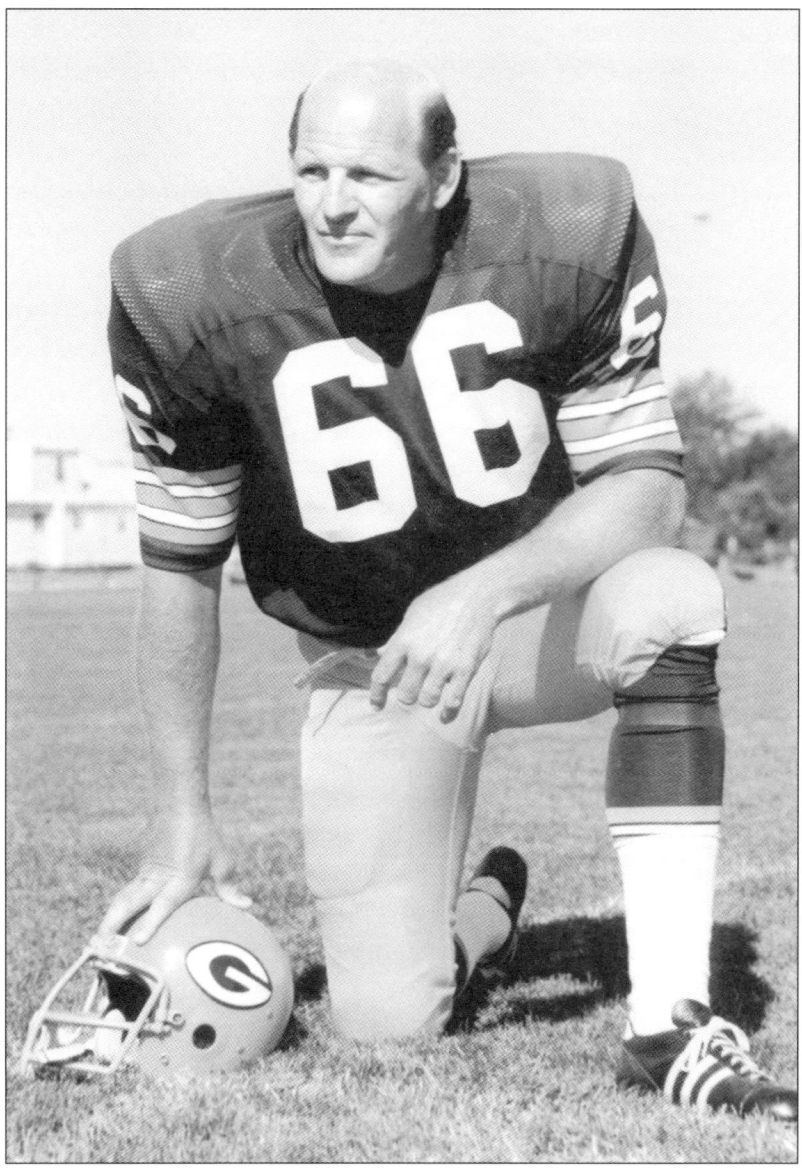

Ray Nitschke – Overcoming self-destruction to become the best linebacker in Packer history.

Packer Hall of Fame photo

day would come when I'd have to make this announcement, it never really is an easy one to do. You can prepare yourself for it, but I'm going to retire. After 15 years and another summer camp, I'm going to hang up the number 66 for the last time.

The spirit I have is still there, but the numbers game got me. There's no room on the roster for a third middle linebacker, so I'm retiring.

"Really, it's one of the hardest decisions that I've ever had to make, but every good thing must some day come to an end, and so must my football playing days.

"As I look back, I have to look on Ray Nitschke as one of the most fortunate athletes to ever play the game. I want to thank all of my past and present teammates and everyone in the Packer organization for their help. And the fans who have backed me so loyally throughout my career, Man, they have been great. No athlete has had the support I have had and I'm really proud of it."

Nitschke made an easy transition to life off the field. He continued to live in the Green Bay area. He wrote for the *Packer Report*, was an America's Pack fan club spokesman and he became an accomplished speaker and able pitchman for various projects and products, most notably his television commercials for Miller Lite beer. For almost a quarter century, he ably marketed himself, making countless appearances, hosting cruises, attending card shows and helping with charities.

Nitschke's popularity actually grew after his retirement. When introduced at a game at Lambeau, he and Bart Starr always got the loudest ovations.

Tom Murphy, director and archivist for the Green Bay Packer Hall of Fame told me, "We all remember Ray Nitschke. His name will live on as long as there is football played in Green Bay. He will be remembered not only for what he accomplished on the football field, but also for the caring human being that he was. His demeanor was just a front for a very caring person with a big heart.

"After his wife, Jackie, passed away, Ray didn't seem to

enjoy life quite as much. Calling our house one time, he broke down when my wife, Kathy, asked him how he was getting along. His wife had been so instrumental in getting him to stop drinking and settling down.

"Now he was alone. It was shortly thereafter that Ray died of a heart attack while wintering in Florida. I saw him a few weeks before he died and he introduced me to some people as his 'good buddy'. That meant a lot. Ray was the kind of person you wanted to be associated with. He was always there for local charities and he especially helped me with projects at the Green Bay Packer Hall of Fame. All of us who were privileged to know him still miss him."

As a sportswriter Bud Lea, who covered the Packers for years, wrote, "Whatever it was that made Ray Nitschke whatever he was, he was one-of-a-kind. He loved being with the Packers and their fans, and they loved him."

Ray died of a sudden heart attack in 1998, two years after Jackie's death. But Packer fans will never forget the young wild-man who became a loving and caring man, and who also would become the best linebacker in the NFL's first 50 years.

Fred 'Fuzzy' Thurston

Conquering adversity off the field – an inspirational story.

Fred 'Fuzzy' Thurston was an All-Pro guard for the Lombardi teams of the 1960's. For the most part, he escaped serious football injuries during the nine years he played for the Packers. However, his off-the-field adversities and hardships were substantial. The manner in which Fuzzy overcame these life-altering situations is nothing short of inspirational.

Early in life, growing up in stark poverty in a small town in northwestern Wisconsin, Fuzzy was the only one of seven children who didn't have to quit to help earn money for the family, and therefore, was able to graduate from high school. Tragically, Fuzzy lost his father when he was four, requiring his mother to go it alone for much of his childhood.

Then, not playing any organized football until he was a junior in a small college in Indiana, Fuzzy overcame huge odds to become one of the most honored guards in the NFL. However, adversity hit him hard a few years after retirement from the Packers. His restaurant business hit tough times, folded and forced him into bankruptcy. He and his wife, Sue, lost everything.

Finally, his most severe catastrophe hammered him

when he was diagnosed with cancer nearly 26 years ago. Long, drawn out treatments and two surgeries finally left Fuzzy with no vocal cords. He had lost his ability to talk.

It's hard to believe, but those who know Fuzzy best – including most of his Packer teammates of the 1960's – say through all of his trials and tribulations, he is still optimistic, upbeat, and always of good cheer, a kind of courage that is rare indeed.

Fuzzy grew up and went to high school in Altoona, Wisconsin, a small town near Eau Claire, with at that time, a population of 1,000. After his father died, his mother raised their seven children with the help of the older children, until she married again ten years later.

They lived in an old two-story house on a dirt road next to the railroad tracks. Fuzzy got used to doing with the bare necessities. When he was eleven, Fuzzy was sent to live with an aunt in Florida. It was one less mouth for his mother to feed.

Thurston's mother, strong-minded and necessarily strict, also gave her children love and some good advise. Fuzzy recalled, "My mother was instrumental in making me aware of how difficult life could be. She told me to be happy as long as I have food on the table and a family to love. Life was very simple, but it wasn't easy. In fact, it was very difficult. It was still enjoyable, though, and my mother made it that way. I'm so grateful for what my mother taught me. I learned how to be happy and stay strong in whatever circumstances I was faced with."

When Fuzzy got back from his one year in Florida, he began to shoot baskets at a hoop at a nearby gas station. Day after day, month after month, he shot away – either by himself or with his friends.

Since his high school did not field a football team, basketball became his passion. By the time he entered high school, he was a good shot from almost any spot on the floor and he took over the guard position on his high school's basketball team. As a 155-pound senior, Fuzzy had become one of the best basketball players in Altoona's conference.

PROFILES OF COURAGE • FUZZY THURSTON

Fred "Fuzzy" Thurston was an All-Pro guard for the Lombardi teams of the 1960s. For the most part he escaped serious football injuries during the nine years he played for the Packers. However, his off-the-field adversities and hardships were substantial. The manner in which Fuzzy overcame these life-altering situations is nothing short of inspirational.

Packer Hall of Fame photo

Thurston has his own recollection of his days in Altoona, "Looking back on growing up in Altoona, I was just the average all-American boy. By average, I mean just that. Average. I wasn't great at anything!"

He was good enough, however, to get invited to play basketball at Valparaiso, a small college in northern Indiana, where he played during both his freshman and sophomore years.

But then football entered his life. Now stocky and strong, at 230 pounds, but still light on his feet, an assistant football coach convinced Fuzzy to try to go out for the football team.

Fuzzy remembered, "I was nineteen years old. I had never played organized football, except for some sandlot football while growing up in Altoona, but I had always liked sports. It's just that I had spent twelve months out of the year practicing basketball, so it was the only sport I really knew how to play."

He ended up playing three years in the offensive line at Valparaiso and made the All-Conference team. He was named 'Most Valuable Player' of the conference his last season. He spent the summer of 1956 building up his strength, doing tough construction work. It was also the summer he met and began to date his future wife, Sue.

The Philadelphia Eagles thought enough of him to draft Fuzzy in the fourth round of the college draft the following spring. His stay with the Eagles was short. "I never played that final exhibition game because the Eagles cut me. I was so hurt and so down, and I was staring at two years of military duty. Somehow, I kept my spirits up because I still believed I would make it in the NFL. It was never a matter of whether I could play. It was only a question of when," Fuzzy said.

Now married, Thurston went back home to Altoona, opened his mail to find his Army draft notice, and left a few weeks later for the service. In the end, his experience in the military proved invaluable. In addition to his assigned duties, he wrestled and played football as left tackle for the Army.

During the next 21 months, he honed his skills, polished his technique, and absorbed a great deal of football knowledge.

The quality of football was better than he had seen at Valparaiso, probably on par with the Big Ten, but not nearly as good as the NFL. By the time his hitch was up, he had made a name for himself and was fairly respected by other NFL players in the service.

One player he met in the Army was Chicago Bears' end, Harlon Hill, who helped Fuzzy sign with the Bears in 1958. In the middle of their exhibition season, they traded Fuzzy back to the Eagles, who cut him at the end of the exhibition season.

After a short tour with the Winnipeg Blue Bombers, he signed with the Baltimore Colts and spent six weeks on their taxi squad. As fate would have it, when he was activated, his first game was against the Packers. The Colts crushed Green Bay, 56-0, went on to a 9-3 season and beat the Giants in the now famous televised championship game, 23-17. The Packers finished with the worst record in their history at 1-10-1.

Feeling great about being on a World Championship team, Fuzzy was about to get another surprise. Just before training camp started in 1959, he was traded by the Colts to the Packers. Fuzzy recalled how he felt at the time – going from champs to chumps: "On the drive from Baltimore back to Wisconsin, I thought, 'This is going to be my home. Please God, no more. I've been around. I've done it. I've paid the price. Let me be here and stay here.

"By the time I hit the Maryland state line, I had adjusted my perspective, finding all the good in what started out as a major disappointment. I was the happiest guy in the world. I was going to see my wife, Susan, and our beautiful family that included a newborn son. I was going to be playing for the team I had loved while I was growing up. I wasn't going to be a loser. I was coming home. It was just a matter of rearranging my attitude and my expectations, and it was going to be all right. In fact, it was going to be fantastic."

In Fuzzy Thurston's first training camp, in 1959, he was continually hurt. "Damn it, Fuzzy! If you don't play today, you're going home!" Coach Lombardi hollered. "You're always hurt! You're always complaining!" Thurston became furious. "I'll show that son-of-a-bitch," he said, and he tore off his bandages, played, made the squad, and eventually started. (*Milwaukee Journal*)

When he got to the Packer locker room for the first time, the first person he ran into was the new coach, Vince Lombardi. Fuzzy remembers it well, "He sized me up from across the empty locker room, with those dark, penetrating eyes. He wasted no time issuing a question that sounded more like a challenge. 'Who the hell are you?' he shouted.

Fuzzy recalls, "My new teammates had just left the locker room to hit the practice field for the morning workout, so, I figured this was as good a time as any to introduce myself. 'Coach, I'm Fuzzy Thurston," I said. 'You're late,' he said in an intimidating voice. 'You should've been here yesterday! Don't let that happen again!'"

Fuzzy went on to become an integral member of one of the most celebrated teams in professional sports. He helped the Packers win an unprecedented five World Championships and two Super Bowls. He was voted 'All-Pro' for three consecutive seasons, and in 1962, received more All-Pro votes than any other NFL player.

Thurston and teammate Jerry Kramer were named the best guard combination in the first 50 years of professional football. In 1975, Fuzzy was inducted into the Packers Hall of Fame, and in 2003, he was inducted into the Wisconsin Athletic Hall of Fame.

"Fuzzy always lived his life as if it might end tomorrow. He jammed everything into it, relished every minute. He was always charging, always up. How are things, Fuzz? Fantastic! Sensational! Terrific! Every day, he was like a little boy at Christmas," Paul Horning once wrote. "Fuzzy is quite the opposite of Jerry. He is a fun-loving guy off the

PROFILES OF COURAGE • FUZZY THURSTON

Fuzzy (r) and teammate Jerry Kramer (l) were named best guard combination in the first 50 years of professional football.

Packer Hall of Fame photo

"It's amazing how Fuzzy still lights up a room."
  Bill Wenzel,
  Friend and business partner
  Thurston Collection photo

Fuzy and his wife Sue now live in Waupaca, Wisconsin. A 40-minute drive from Green Bay.
  Thurston Collection photo

field and a monster on. He has probably got the greatest recuperative powers of anybody I've seen. He played over a hundred straight games and that's pretty good, especially when you're playing line." (*Football and the Single Man*)

After his retirement, Thurston began to expand the restaurant business he had started a few years earlier with a couple of partners, including teammate Max McGee. Left Guard restaurants began to pop up all over Wisconsin in the 1960's. By the early 1970's, a slower economy and higher interest rates caught up with Fuzzy's optimistic nature.

He ended up closing some Left Guards, but not fast enough. Thurston was forced into bankruptcy and lost his house, cottage, and cars – in short – everything he and Sue owned. He was flat broke. Some loyal friends helped them the next few years. He opened another restaurant in Neenah and began to get back to normal when he got hit with more bad news.

Thurston was diagnosed with cancer of the vocal cords. When he got the word from the doctor, he walked outside and wept. Surgery, six months of radiation, and Fuzzy's ambitious exercise program led to the doctor's claim the cancer was in remission.

"When I first returned home after surgery, I tried to write down questions and answers to communicate. I would write out a question to someone and one of two things would happen. They would either write their response, forgetting that I could hear just fine, or start talking really loud, as if I were deaf. I can't help but laugh about it now, but it didn't seem that funny at the time," Fuzzy recalled.

Fuzzy thought he might be in the clear again, but not so. One year later, a checkup showed the cancer had returned. One more surgery took out his only remaining vocal cord and his larynx. Fuzzy was now rendered speechless.

Fuzzy remembered how he tried to handle the situation. "It was terrible. I started to work really hard on being able to communicate. I would practice talking in front of the mirror. It was painful both physically and emotionally. I was scheduled to see a speech therapist to learn how to talk again. I only went once because I had already started to teach myself. At first, I couldn't say anything. When I finally got a sound out, I felt like celebrating. It took a lot of work. I kept practicing and praying."

Nearly 23 years have now passed and his cancer is still in remission. Although he has had both hips replaced twice, Thurston remains thankful. "I was glad to be alive and to have a second chance. I could have drowned in my own self pity, and almost did for brief moments on really bad days, but I refuse to quit," Fuzzy said.

He now owns another restaurant and bar he calls 'Fuzzy's 63' in Green Bay, in the shadows of Lambeau Field. While he and Sue live in Waupaca, a 40-minute drive from Green Bay, 'Fuzzy's 63' is his favorite hangout. You'll find him there on Packer home games and often in between, except in the winter, when he and Sue are in Florida. He also runs 'Fuzzy Thurston's Titletown Tickets and Tours.'

Now in his mid-70's, he still stays in touch with most of his Packer teammates of the 1960's and is still his optimistic, cheerful self. Bill Wenzel, a business partner, said, "Its amazing how Fuzzy still lights up a room. Fans still love him. He will sign every request for an autograph. He can talk a little when he presses against his throat, but he doesn't need to speak – his wonderful personality shines from his face and smile."

In 2006, Thurston wrote a book titled, What a Wonderful Life. It's basically his life story. If you read the book you will get the sense it's a nice long letter from Fuzzy, along with many of his favorite pictures.

Fuzzy sums up his feelings about his life this way:

"I believe that fate plays an important role in life. Many things are simply out of our control. What we can control is how we react to life's adversities and challenges. I believe the lessons I learned from the role models in my life have helped me overcome challenges. My mother always taught me to appreciate what you have, not what you don't have. My wife, Sue, reinforced that belief during my battles with cancer and bankruptcy.

"I believe that my ability to fight and overcome these challenges is also a reflection on Coach Lombardi. He taught me about the will required to persevere through tough times and the discipline required to succeed. Coach Lombardi had a famous saying, 'The will to win, will to succeed, these are the things that endure.' Coach Lombardi was right. He taught me never to quit, and I never will."

Willie Wood

Overcoming extreme odds as a Packer walk-on to make it all the way to the Pro Football Hall of Fame

Rising from being a player no one wanted, to achieving almost every honor in the NFL, including the prestigious pinnacle, the Pro Football Hall of Fame, Willie Wood epitomizes the underdog who proves he belongs, given the opportunity.

When Willie Wood graduated from the University of Southern California in 1959, it was hard for him to realize, no pro team wanted him enough to include him in the college draft.

Even though he had been the starting quarterback and defensive back for three years for the USC Trojans and he desperately wanted to play in the pros, no NFL team thought he was good enough. "When I got out of SC, " he said, "I had two strikes on me." He was the wrong color, a Black quarterback when the NFL had no Black quarterbacks, and he was the wrong size. "I was the only one who thought I had a chance, " Willie said.

When the draft was held, Willie was passed over. During that time, each of the 12 teams had 30 draft picks. NFL teams saw him as an injured – he had broken his collar bone senior year – undersized, 5'-10", Black quarterback.

Determined to get his shot at the pros, Willie started writing to pro clubs asking for at least a tryout. He thought he could be a pretty good defensive back.

Other teams didn't bother to answer, or gave him polite brush-off. In Green Bay, however, the Lombardi era was starting. And one thing Coach Vince Lombardi wanted was a defensive back.

The late Jack Vainisi, then Green Bay talent scout, offered to pay Wood's transportation to the Packers' camp in Green Bay for a tryout. Once he got there, it didn't take the diminutive Wood long to make an impression.

Wood made a strong first impression in practice when he laid out Jim Taylor with a solid tackle. Lombardi ordered the play run to be repeated, and Willie dropped the larger Taylor again. Lombardi and the whole team were impressed with this little man's toughness.

Bart Starr recalled, "It took Willie about ten minutes to realize we had somebody special. He could jump higher than anyone else, he out-hustled everyone on special team, covered receivers like a blanket, and returned punts better than anyone we had on the team."

Wood recalled that first year in 1960. "I really thought my chances to make the team were slim to none. I kept my mouth shut. Lombardi was tough and I thought he yelled a lot. I tried to play as hard as I could and stay out of his way. Lombardi knew I was small, but I had large shoulders and a seventeen-inch neck. Lombardi like that."

Lombardi certainly liked something. Willie made the team. "I don't think I could have made it with any other team, or any other coach," he said.

Wood did make the Packers team as a safety in 1960 and proved he belonged in the NFL. In his twelve years with the Packers, Willie had 48 career interceptions, second only to team leader, Bobby Dillion, and is still the all-time team leader in most punt returns (187).

The NFL reject was named All Pro six consecutive seasons, went to eight straight Pro Bowls and received the highest honor any pro player can obtain, when he was

Profiles of Courage • WILLIE WOOD

Willie Wood (24) gets a block from Elijah Pitts (22) on a punt return. Wood played with the Packers from 1960 through 1971. Willie still holds the Packer career record for total punt returns (187) and total return yards (1,391).

Milwaukee Journal photo

elected to the Pro Football Hall of Fame in 1989. Wood was also inducted into the Packer Hall of Fame in 1977, six years after his retirement. Jerry Kramer, Wood's teammate, said, "Willie deserved to be elected to the Pro Football Hall of Fame. His credentials were every bit as impressive as Herb Adderley's, and his reputation for ferocity, for tackling hard, was unmatchable. All of our guys hit hard, but Willie hit extra hard.

"Pound for pound," Coach Lombardi said, "Willie, who filled out to 190, was the best tackler in the game." And all because of Willie's initial determination and Lombardi's willingness to give him a chance.

Willie grew up in Washington, DC, where his mother and father both worked for the federal government. He went west to college, starting at Coalinga Junior College in California's San Joaquin Valley, before ending up at the University of Southern California. At USC, Wood was a three-year letterman as a running quarterback. His position coach was Al Davis, future owner of the Raiders.

In 1960, Willie played mostly on special teams and as backup to the starter, the great Em Tunnel, who was getting close to retirement. Tunnel, who had been the premier free safety in the league throughout the 1950's and would be the first Black inducted into the Hall of Fame, was a generous individual who became both roommate and mentor to Wood. Willie would later say, "Em taught me everything."

In 1960, his rookie season, Wood was a reserve. He drew his first attention as a punt return specialist, leading the league by sidestepping would-be tacklers time after time. "He runs faster sideways than most people do frontward," said one amazed scout sitting in the Green Bay press box.

Willie's first game in defense came in the sixth game of the 1960 season and he didn't get off to a good start. However, it came against the best – Johnny Unitas and the Baltimore Colts. Starter Jesse Whittenton got hurt and Willie was inserted at left cornerback against All Pro receiver Raymond Berry.

Wood repeatedly was beaten, and was eventually

PROFILES OF COURAGE • WILLIE WOOD

Willie Wood, the Packers walk-on who made it all the way to Pro Football Hall of Fame.

Packer Hall of Fame photo

replaced that day by Dick Pesonen. After the game, Wood was badly shaken and uncertain about his future, when Lombardi took him aside and told him to shake it off because he was going to be here as long as the coach was going to be in Green Bay.

In 1961, Willie won the starting free safety position, replacing the aging Tunnel, and the Packers won their first title in 17 years. He intercepted five passes and led the league in punt returns with a 16.1 average. He took back two punts for touchdowns.

The next year, he led the NFL with nine interceptions and averaged 11.9 yards per punt return. He also kicked off for the team. Unfortunately, he was ejected from the 1962 title game when he jumped up quickly to protest a penalty call and accidentally bumped into the official. The most memorable moment of his career came in the first Super Bowl.

Willie turned the game around early in the second half. The Chiefs' quarterback, Len Dawson, was rushed by the Packers' front four and thrown off-balance. Wood intercepted the fluttering pass and ran 40 yards to the Chiefs' five-yard line, where Pitts took it in for a 21-10 lead.

Kramer, in his book, *Distant Replay*, wrote, "Willie's career lasted twelve seasons, all of them in Green Bay. He probably would have been better off if he had left after nine, if in 1969, he had accompanied Lombardi to Washington, to his hometown. Willie knew by then he wanted to coach, and Vince had encouraged him. He would have loved to have served an apprenticeship under Lombardi. But in 1969, Willie was still skilled enough to be chosen for the Pro Bowl. The Packers were not about to let him go."

After his retirement as a player in 1971, Willie was defensive backs coach in San Diego before becoming the first Black head coach of a professional football team with the Philadelphia Bell in the World Football League in 1975. The Bell had a losing record that year, before the entire league folded. Willie got a second chance in the Canadian Football League when he took over the Toronto Argonauts from his former teammate, Forrest Gregg, in 1980. Argos went 6-20 over the next two seasons and Wood was fired.

Wood left football for business at that point and moved back to his hometown of Washington, DC. He still returns to Green Bay to watch the Packers from time to time. He was elected to the Packer Hall of Fame in 1977, and his induction to the Pro Football Hall of Fame occurred in 1989.

Now, over 70 years old and crippled with painful arthritis in his knees, back and hips, Willie has tried to stay active during his retirement years. Since he has come on hard times financially, several former teammates have come forward to help him. He now has to get around mostly in a wheelchair. Willie has been married twice, but both women are deceased. He stays in touch with his two children, daughter, Lawan, and his son, Willie, Jr., who manages singers while living in Chicago.

Willie also remains in contact with some of his teammates from the 1960's – primarily Herb Adderley, Bob Jeter and Tom Brown – all defensive backs during that period. And he remembers when he had the courage to pursue his dream, when no one but the Packers thought he was good enough.

The 1962 Season

Team Courage on Display

The Packers' 1962 Season chosen as a prime example of 'team courage.'

Many sportswriters, rival coaches, and former Packer players, themselves, call the 1962 Packers the best team in the history of the NFL. The 1962 Packers were 13-1, finished first in the Western Conference, and led the NFL in scoring. They outscored their opponents 415 to 148 and then whipped the Giants, again, for the World Championship.

Jim Taylor led the league in rushing and rushing touchdowns, while Bart Starr ranked first among quarterbacks. Willie Wood, All-Pro defensive back during that year, said, "We were a great team in 1962."

Ray Nitschke called it, "...the best team ever – no argument."

It's our premise that the 1962 season took the boldness, spirit and special courage of an entire team, not just a small handful of players. But first, a flashback of two years.

Green Bay's 1960 season began the most successful and astonishing eight-year period in the Packers' long, legendary history. This magical timeframe was set up in 1959, when Vince Lombardi coached the team to its first winning record in eleven long years, and it best record in fourteen seasons.

He took over a club that had had only one win, a tie, and ten losses, in 1958, and turned it into an immediate winner, 7-5. But the best was yet to come. It was almost unbelievable to faithful Packer fans, almost too good to be true. After nearly sixteen years of mediocre, losing football, the Packers won their last two games of the 1960 season to capture the NFL Western Conference championship. It was too glorious to comprehend.

It was toward the end of Vince Lombardi's winning season with the Packers, in 1960, when rumors began that the coach would be going back to New York. It was said the New York Giants were going to lure Lombardi back as their head coach. Everyone knew how Lombardi missed the 'Big Apple.' He loved New York. He grew up in Brooklyn, went to school in the Bronx, and began coaching just across the river in New Jersey. It was in New York that he had made his debut as assistant coach with the Giants before coming to Green Bay. Although he had been welcomed in Green Bay and had quickly became a Wisconsin god, it seemed an opportune time for Lombardi to jump at an offer from the Giants.

But he stayed in Green Bay, and in two short years of unparalleled success, the Packers' board had turned the club over to Lombardi, lock, stock, and barrel. He had struck fear and respect for excellence not only into his players, but also into everyone in the front office, including the board members. His demand for excellence ran all the way from the field to the locker room. He had total control – but was also earning undying respect from everyone.

The next season would be even better. On a bitter, cold New Year's Eve in 1961, the Green Bay Packers completely dominated the New York Giants, 37-0, on Lambeau Field, then still called City Stadium. It was the first of five NFL championships for the Vince Lombardi-coached Packers.

The Packers played a nearly flawless game. It was football, about as perfect as it could be executed. Paul Hornung remembered the Packer locker room after the game, "In the dressing room before he let anyone in, Coach Lombardi made a little speech. You could see he was moved. He kept wiping at his glasses. He said, 'Today, you were the greatest team in the history of the National Football League.'"

A record-breaking 55 million viewers watched the game on television and witnessed a team that Lombardi had prepared for perfection. It was a frightening display of one team completely dominating. Green Bay went berserk. Automobiles were still tooting their horns at two in the morning.

While the people of Green Bay celebrated until late in the night, the Packer dynasty of the 1960's had begun in a most convincing manner. Before the 1962 exhibition season, Vince was unusually candid with reporters about his team's prospects. He told the Green Bay *Press-Gazette*, "I have to be truthful and say that we've got a pretty solid football team. I also have to say that we're the team to beat." Nonetheless, Vince remained watchful for complacency, staleness, and poor execution. Before the season, he again publicly warned his players against 'fatheadedness.'

As it turned out, Lombardi also co-authored a book with W.C. Heinz covering the 1962 season by focusing on one week and one game that year. The book, *Run to Daylight*, was an enormous success when it came out in the fall of 1963. It made the 1962 season the most celebrated and popular during Lombardi's tenure.

The Packers blew through the pre-season exhibition games, winning all six, under the constant prodding of Lombardi. He was concerned the players would start to get puffed up after winning the NFL Championship in 1961. Lombardi let up only slightly from his boot camp approach in previous pre-season training camps. Jerry Kramer said, "Vince still rode us unmercifully, pouncing upon every slight imperfection."

There was still an emphasis on conditioning and running plays over and over again to achieve perfection. Lombardi still had no tolerance for players' minor injuries or for underachievers. He'd say, "Learn to play hurt – it's the nature of the game." Most players cranked it up a notch or two to meet Lombardi's expectations.

The Packers would have an early season advantage, playing their first four games on home fields in Green Bay and Milwaukee. The opening game against the talent-thick Vikings was a mismatch. The Packers won in a cakewalk, 34-7. The second game of the season, held in Milwaukee County Stadium, was a bit tighter, but the Packers still won with a strong defensive effort, 17-0, over the St. Louis Cardinals. Jimmy Taylor ran up the middle, around end, through tackle or up the middle of St. Louis' line 23 times for 122 yards behind the Packers' scythe-like blocking.

The following Sunday, the Packers met the Chicago Bears, who came into the game undefeated. When the Bears left City stadium, they were not just defeated, they were humiliated. The Packers hammered the Bears, 49-0. It was the widest margin of victory between the two oldest NFL teams, in their 87th meeting.

The game was such a one-sided rout that Lombardi felt he had to make some kind of an apology. In the locker room after the game, he said, "I feel badly about it. We didn't try to do it (run up the score.)"

Bears coach, George Halas, was a bit more realistic when he told reporters after the game, "The Packers were just too good today. They are a great team."

The Packers did look like a great team after their first three games. They had outscored their opponents, 100-7. Only the Vikings had scored on them, and that was a fluke touchdown pass in the last seconds of the game. The Milwaukee and Green Bay press began talk of an undefeated season. Lombardi, when questioned about going through the season with no losses, angrily said, "I don't like that talk. It's a long season."

The following Sunday was to be a showdown between the NFL's two best teams – the Packers and the Detroit Lions – both with 3-0 records. The Lions had finished second to Green Bay in 1961. They were a talented and hungry team.

It rained, off and on, for most of the week before the

PROFILES OF COURAGE • 1962 SEASON

Left: Paul Hornung runs for a touchdown against the Vikings. He scored the first 20 points in the Packers' 34-7 win.
UPI Beltman News photo

Fifty-nine and a half minutes of frustration are wiped out in a twinkling and the Green Bay Packer bench goes wild as Paul Hornung boots a field goal to beat the Lions. The "head cheerleader," Max McGee, has run out on the field. Left (on field) are Herb Adderley and rookie Ed Blaine (#60). Holding his helmet is star fullback Jim Taylor and at right is defensive end Bill Quinlan.
Milwaukee Journal photo

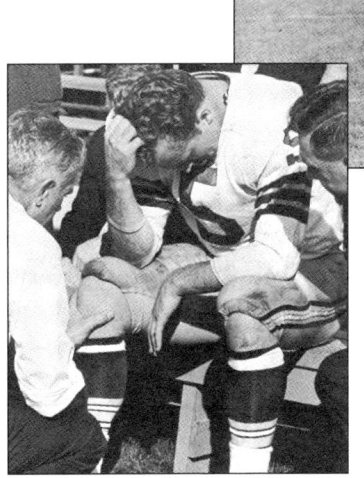

Hornung, who suffered a serious knee injury in a 1962 game against the Minnesota Vikings, played sparingly for the rest of the year.
Wide World photo

game, setting a gloomy tone for practice. Lombardi told Heinz he had hardly slept all week. He was a nervous wreck. It rained again on game day, which created a wet, slippery, muddy field. The game was televised, rare in those days, while a full house of 38,000 crammed into City Stadium (now Lambeau Field).

What everyone witnessed was a grueling, grind-it-out defensive battle. After nearly four quarters of play, the Lions led, 7-6. The Packers' offense struggled, as Taylor was sick but playing with a 101-degree fever, and Hornung was playing hurt. With less than two minutes left, the Lions had the ball with third and eight on their 49-yard line. It looked like it was over. If the Lions ran another play and punted deep in Packer territory, it looked like too much to overcome. Fans began to file out of City Stadium.

But wait! The Lions' Milt Plum went back to pass and his left foot slipped a bit as he threw. He aimed at Terry Barr, his gifted receiver, but he also slipped just as he cut for the pass. The Packers' Herb Adderley cut in front of Barr, intercepted, and ran 41 yards to the Lion 17. After two short-yardage running plays, Hornung kicked a 13-yard field goal through the gloom and mist for a 9-7 win.

In the Packer dressing room, Lombardi choked up while the players chanted "Herb! Herb!"

Milwaukee Journal writer, Terry Bledsoe, said the Packer victory was brought about by only one thing. "I attribute it to Lombardi's will," he said. The Packers, now 4-0, traveled to Minneapolis and trampled all over the Vikings again. This time the score was 48-21.

After the first five games of the 1962, season, the Packers had completely dominated their opponents, with the exception of the close 9-7 win over the tough Detroit Lions. Standing at 5-0 and in first place in the Western Division, Green Bay had outscored opponents, 157-35. The Packers were the highest-scoring team in the NFL and their stout defense had allowed the fewest points. However, some of the players were experiencing injuries.

After Green Bay's 48-21 win over the Vikings in game

five, Lombardi learned Paul Hornung would probably miss several of the next games with a serious knee injury. At that point in the season, Hornung was the NFL's leading scorer and the Packers' second-leading ground gainer. He was also one of the team's better receivers and did all the team's kicking.

The Packers met the San Francisco 49ers in game six and started the game off slowly. Trailing 13-10 early in the third quarter, the Packers exploded with a 21-point blast to wrap up their sixth-straight victory, 31-13.

The Packers traveled to Baltimore to meet the up-and-down Colts (3-3) for game seven. The Colts were not the same team since their championship seasons a few years earlier, but were still solid, with Hall-of-Fame quarterback Johnny Unitas, halfback Tom Matte, receivers Raymond Berry (who was bothered by a bad knee), Jimmy Orr and R.G. Owens.

In a close, smash-mouthed game, on a sunny Sunday afternoon, the Packers held a slim 10-6 lead midway through the fourth quarter, when Ray Nitschke's interception pulled the Packers out of the hole in which they had been, and led directly to the clinching touchdown in their 17-6 victory over the Colts.

Reminded that it was quite an accomplishment to win seven in a row, Lombardi agreed that it was an accomplishment, but quickly turned his thoughts to the future – the next seven – saying, "Each game will get a lot tougher, and we'll be fighting for our lives. There are no easy ones."

What started out as a close defensive game on a cold, windy Sunday in Chicago, with the Packers holding a narrow 10-7 lead early in the second half, broke wide open when Green Bay scored four touchdowns in the last 22 minutes for a 38-7 win. It was their eighth in a row.

Bears tight end, Mike Ditka, complimented the Packers after the game. "They're the greatest – absolutely the greatest. The Packers have the confidence. In their own minds, they can't be beaten."

After the game, Hornung, still out with an injured knee,

which hadn't healed enough to play, took his date to King's, a favorite Packer restaurant in Green Bay. Having had a couple martinis, and being in a foul mood because he hadn't been playing, Hornung hit a guy for making a wisecrack about the 'Golden Boy' just outside the restaurant door before going in.

Hornung would remember in his new book, *Lombardi and Me*, "As he walked up to me, I put my 1961 championship ring on my ring hand. When he got close enough and started to say something, I swung and hit him." After a few blows, with the two of them wrestling around on the ground, Ron Kramer rushed out of the restaurant and broke it up. Hornung later admitted it had been a stupid move on his part, and he was grateful it had never made the papers.

The Packers traveled to Philadelphia's Franklin Field looking for their ninth consecutive win. They were also seeking redemption for their loss on that same field to the Eagles in the 1960 championship game. With that little extra incentive, Green Bay crushed the over-matched Eagles, 49-0. After the game, the Eagles' great receiver, Tommy McDonald said, "The question has been asked, who's going to catch Green Bay? I don't know if anyone *wants* to catch Green Bay."

The Packers now entered the most critical stage of the 1962 season, going after their tenth straight victory, against the Colts in Green Bay. It would be the Packers' first of two games against contenders within five days. The Colts, now with a 5-4 record, were tied with Chicago for third place. The following Thursday, Thanksgiving Day, the Packers would meet the Lions (7-2) in Detroit.

A full house of 38,000 crammed into City Stadium on a beautiful Wisconsin fall afternoon in anticipation of a classic football game. They were not disappointed. But it was a game in which the Packers began to look 'human.' Call it luck, fortune, or simply a display of unusual courage, the Packers remained undefeated. Lombardi's so-far-invincible legions defeated the Colts, 17-13, for their tenth-straight victory. They were outgained on the ground and in the air, and the Colts had three times as many first downs (19 to 6), so to accomplish their objective, they had to come up with three critical defensive goal line stands that were just this side of amazing.

The Colts had first down on the Packer one and couldn't score. They also got inside the Packer ten with a first down and settled for a field goal. Finally, the Colts had first and goal on the Packer seven and failed to score.

As it turned out, the Packers had just enough offense. In the first quarter, Herb Adderley ran back a kickoff 103 yards for a touchdown. Tom Moore, Hornung's back-up, ran off tackle for 23-yards and a touchdown in the fourth quarter. Jerry Kramer also kicked a 24-yard field goal in the first quarter – not much, but enough.

After the narrow win over the Baltimore Colts, the Packers were now 10-0 and in first place in the Western Conference of the NFL. Their archrivals in the 1960's, the Detroit Lions, were right behind Green Bay at 8-2.

Although intent on winning, Lombardi was becoming irritated with the media constantly asking him about the team going undefeated. He reminded the players not to get inflated egos with that kind of talk.

Lombardi especially hammered on it the days before the Packers' next critical game against the Lions in Detroit on Thanksgiving Day. He knew the Lions were bent on revenge for the defeat they had suffered in their first meeting. Every Detroit player and coach felt the Packers had gotten 'lucky' in their last-second 9-7 win in Green Bay. Nearly 60,000 crammed into Tiger Stadium on a wet, overcast day, eager to see their beloved Lions rip apart the champion Packers. They would not be disappointed.

The Packers were practically devoured by the aroused Lions. The 26-14 score was terribly misleading. The Packers trailed 26-0 going into the fourth quarter when they scored two touchdowns on fluke plays.

Detroit's pumped up defense resembled a group of starved, mad dogs as they tore through the Packers' offensive line, play after play. They either crushed the ball carriers in their tracks or whipped Starr into the ground when he went back to pass. 'Awesome' hardly describes the Lions' overpowering defense and total domination of the game. It would go down in Packer history as Lombardi's most humbling defeat.

However, you would never have known it when the reporters converged on Lombardi after the loss in the stadium locker room. Lombardi seemed to be in a surprisingly good mood. He greeted the press with his big, toothy smile as though the Packers had won.

"What can I do for you gentlemen?" asked the coach of the defending World Champions, who had just been kicked apart by the second place Lions. "Ask and I shall answer."

It was plain to see that the lid was off, that the pressure of the 10-game winning streak (12, counting the two at the end of 1961) had finally been released, like unlocking the door on a steam chamber, and for that relief at least, Lombardi was happy.

After the Detroit massacre, Lombardi and his coaches regrouped for a meeting with the last place Los Angeles Rams (1-9-1). Having been embarrassed by Detroit on national television, the Rams would be the ideal team for the Packers to play against to regain their edge for the remaining three games in their quest for their third straight Western Conference championship.

A full house would fill up Milwaukee County Stadium on an unseasonably warm Sunday to watch the Packers whip the Rams with relative ease, 41 to 10. The flamboyant halfback, Paul Hornung, returned to the lineup for the first time since injuring his knee against the Vikings back in mid-October and scored early on a 30-yard pass from Starr.

Early the next week, the Packers flew to Palto Alto to prepare for their next game against the improved San Francisco 49ers (6-6). Lombardi called a squad meeting the day they arrived from Green Bay. He impressed upon the players that the 49ers they would meet Sunday were not the same ones they had defeated, 31-13, in Milwaukee earlier in the season. The 49ers now had won three in a row. Even

PROFILES OF COURAGE • 1962 SEASON

Left: In the second half Green Bay recovered somewhat, scoring two touchdowns, but by then it was too late. Here Ray Nitschke (66) and Willie Davis (87) pile on Detroit's Rick Nyder (34).
AP Wire photo

Right: The Packers had no idea how the Lions would whip them on National television on Thanksgiving as they were introduced before the game by Ray Scott. Shown here are Max McGee (85), Fuzzy Thurston (63) and Jim Ringo (51).

Left: Packer halfback Tom Moore goes into air and through a big hole for three yards and a first period touchdown against the Eagles. Number 63 of the Packers is Fred Thurston. Trying to get at Moore is Eagles end Bobby Richards (#68). Tom also scored in the second period on a seven-yard run. He gained 49 yards in 14 carries. The Packers won, 49-0.
AP Wire photo

Right: Against the Colts, the Packers made some tremendous goal line stands. Gremminger and Wood (#24) stop Lenny Moore in his bid for a TD to the right side.

though Green Bay was a 13-point favorite, Lombardi and his staff worked late into the evening in preparation for what they thought could be a tough game.

The improved 49ers did make a game of it for the first half at Kezar Stadium. After 49er quarterback John Brodie picked apart the Packers' usually sturdy defensive backs, San Francisco led the surprised Packers, 21-17, late in the third quarter. Lombardi changed tactics and called for the defense to go to an all-out blitz. The defense tightened and the offense started to get in gear. Starr engineered an 83-yard drive in 12 plays, capped off by Taylor's two-yard touchdown run. Green Bay went ahead for good, 24-21, and won a rough game, 31-21.

After the game, Howard (Red) Hickey, coach of the 49ers, sat on a bench in a crowded, steamy dressing room in Kezar Stadium, sipping a can of liquid refreshment and talking about his team's 31-21 defeat. "The Packers showed why they are a great team today," he said. "They did what a great team has to do – come from behind and win. We were ahead, 21-10, at the half and we had our chances in the second half, but we didn't do it. A lot of teams would have folded with the score 21-10 against them, but not the Packers."

In the Packer locker room, Lombardi stood outside the little visitors' dressing room. He was told what Hickey had said about the Packers not folding. "We never fold," Lombardi said. "We're a tired team right now. This was a long season and there's a lot of pressure being up there week after week, with everyone trying to knock you off."

Quarterback Bart Starr echoed the last statement and got a silent nod of assent from center Jim Ringo. "You should see these teams in the movies of their other games," Starr said, almost indignantly. "They'll play poor football in other games, but against us, they're all great football teams. It's almost unbelievable."

Before the start of the last game of the season against the Rams, the Packers knew the Lions had lost to the Bears, 3-0. Knowing they now had won the Western Conference may have contributed to Green Bay's slow start, as they trailed the Rams, 13-10, at the half. But then Starr warmed up, picking apart the Rams' defense, and came from behind to win, 20-17. Starr finished with 16 of 32 for 205 yards. One of the passes was an 83-yard touchdown to Hornung to put the Packers ahead, 17-13.

The Packers, 31-1, thus concluded the best record in the NFL since the Bears went undefeated, 11-0, in 1942. The win was Green Bay's fifth straight victory over the Rams and boosted Coach Vince Lombardi's four-year league game record to 39-13.

Now the Packers would get ready to meet the New York Giants, 12-2, for the World Championship in two weeks. No two teams belonged together more than the Packers and the Giants, who for the second year in a row, had the two best records in the NFL. The 13-1 Packers led the league in scoring with 415 points, and the 12-2 Giants were second with 398. The Packers had six starters for the West in the Pro Bowl, and the Giants had six starters for the East. While the Giants were installed as three-point favorites, primarily because the game would be played on December 30 in New York's Yankee Stadium, it was the Packers who were the fan favorites.

"The Packers have become news since the Lombardi era," observed Cooper Rollow, explaining why the *Chicago Tribune* had assigned him to cover the Packers. "Now they're big time and as newsworthy as the hometown team in Chicago." During the year, articles on Vince, Green Bay, or star Packer players – particularly Hornung and Taylor – appeared in *Time, Life, Look, The Saturday Evening Post, The New Yorker, The New York Times Magazine, Esquire, Sports, Sports Illustrated*, and *Holiday Magazine*. CBS did a prime time, half-hour special on Lombardi, the team, and the city.

Paul Hornung's ability to go at full strength was still in question. He had started the first five games, but not the next two (Rams and 49ers), and Moore opened the in the last game.

Hornung and the rest of the Packers wanted revenge for the lousy showing they had had on national television on

Thanksgiving Day against Detroit. On the other hand, the Giants were looking for their own revenge for the humiliating 37-0 defeat in the previous year's championship game.

On the day of the game, the temperature was fifteen degrees, but the wind, out of the north at forty miles an hour, made playing conditions atrocious. Nearly 65,000 fans huddled in Yankee Stadium, wearing multiple layers of clothing, trying to ward off the gusty winds. The cold was bitter, while strong winds blew hats and player's overcoats, along with frozen dust across the field. The slick, hard, concrete-like playing field forced the players to wear rubber-soled shoes.

"It was very cold," recalled Gary Knafelc, the Packers' backup receiver. "The wind blew the benches off the field. The field was completely frozen. They had 35-gallon drums with fires burning in them behind the benches."

It was an unspectacular game for the fans in the stands, and the television audience of 43 million was preserved from total dullness only because of the brutal, smash-mouth play on the field by both teams, and the fact the outcome remained in doubt until the last two minutes. The Packers won, but they did not dominate. While the Packers scored in every quarter, they did not put the game away until there were three minutes left to play. Jerry Kramer clinched the game with a 30-yard field goal to make the final score 16-7.

A contest within the game was going on between Taylor and the Giant defenders – particularly linebacker Sam Huff. Taylor said the Giants hurled verbal insults at him all through the game with such choice items as, "You're overrated!" leading the running conversation.

"I just rammed it back down their throats," Taylor said.

In his book, *Game of My Life*, Chuck Carlson quoted Taylor, "In the fourth quarter, we were finally threatening to score. Bart Starr handed it off to me and I went off left tackle. Huff tackled me and said, 'Taylor, you stink.' Then we ran the exact same play, and I ran about seven yards. I skated into the end zone. I held up the ball and said, 'Hey Sam, how do I smell from here?'"

PROFILES OF COURAGE • 1962 SEASON

Packers Jim Taylor scores the only touchdown in Championship game.
AP Wire photo

Willie Wood (24) accidentally knocks down an official.
UPI photo

Big Ray Nitschke (66) deflects a pass from Y. A. Tittle and then both watch as Dan Currie intercepts.

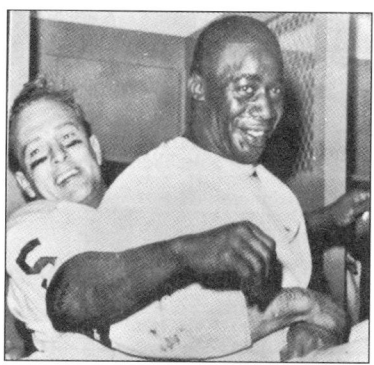 

Paul Hornung gives Wood a victory lift after the game.
UPI photo

Fullback Jim Taylor playfully yanks the tie of guard Jerry Kramer as the pair hoop it up in the Green Bay dressing room at Yankee Stadium. Taylor contributed a touchdown and Kramer booted three field goals.
AP Wire photo

In an early collision with Huff, Taylor bit his tongue and swallowed blood for the rest of the game. By the end, Taylor's arms, elbows, and knees were raw where his flesh had been skinned off.

Afterward, Lombardi was relieved and relaxed as he was hemmed in by an army of reporters in a small cubicle in the catacombs of Yankee Stadium. The game, though, had drained him emotionally; he had difficulty recalling crucial situations and even the final score. "I don't even know the final score," said a confused but happy Lombardi, "All I know is we won, that's all that counts."

Nearly 10,000 screaming fans welcomed the Packers on their return to Green Bay late that night in nine-degrees-below-zero weather. Cars were jammed for the six miles back to the city when the planes touched down at Austin Straubel airport at 10:52 p.m. Many fans en route didn't even reach the air field. Those who reached the airport gave their football heroes a tremendous welcome in a celebration bigger and noisier than a New Year's Eve blast.

Small-town had overwhelmed big-town again, as the incomparable Packers of Green Bay had beaten the Giants of New York for the professional football championship and capped a season of desire and courage by the Packers, that will go down in their history as one of their best ever.

Profiles of Courage • 1962 SEASON

FRONT ROW: (L-R) 22 Elijah Pitts, 60 Ed Blaine, 40 Earl Gros, 80 Gary Barnes, 73 Ron Gassert, 89 Oscar Donahue, 77 Ron Kostelnik. SECOND ROW: (L-R) 24 Willie Wood, 27 John Symank, 46 Hank Gremminger, 58 Dan Currie, 26 Herb Adderley, 61 Nelson Toburen, 10 John Roach, 75 Forrest Gregg. THIRD ROW: (L-R) 51 Jim Ringo, 15 Bart Starr, 84 Gary Knafelc, 64 Jerry Kramer, 63 Fred (Fuzzy) Thurston, 47 Jesse Whittenton, 33 Lew Carpenter, 25 Tom Moore. FOURTH ROW: (L-R) Property Manager Gerald (Dad) Braisher, 76 Bob Skoronski, 66 Ray Nitschke, 53 Ken Iman, 87 Willie Davis, 74 Henry Jordan, Trainer Carl (Bud) Jorgensen. BACK ROW: (L-R) 83 Bill Quinlan, 78 Norm Masters, 86 Boyd Dowler, 31 Jim Taylor, 88 Ron Kramer, 71 Bill Forester, 79 Dave Hanner, 5 Paul Hornung.

Photo courtesy of the Green Bay Packers

Ken Bowman and Larry McCarren

In the center of pain

Too often, football offensive linemen toil in obscurity. Running backs, receivers, quarterbacks on offense and almost every position on the defense get more publicity than the offensive guards, tackles and centers.

Most fans also know more about player injuries, and often, the obstacles they overcome, than they do about the players in the interior of the offensive line. Two Packer players who held down the center position for nearly 20 years displayed the kind of courage it takes to play hurt. That is not too uncommon for interior linemen in the NFL, but not very well known by the average fan. Ken Bowman and Larry McCarren fit that description.

A Rose Bowl starter for the Wisconsin Badgers in 1963, 6'-3", 235-pound Ken Bowman worked his way into the starting center position on the Packer teams of the mid 1960's. Bowman played on three straight championships teams, the first two Super Bowl winners, and the 1972 Central Division champions. He was a Packer from 1964-73.

Bowman followed the Packers' All Pro center in 1964 as the team's starting center. When the Packers drafted Bowman in a low eighth round, they didn't have high expectations. Their starting center, Jim Ringo, one of the best in the NFL, and future Pro Football Hall-of-Famer, had been All-Pro for seven straight seasons.

Bowman, as a rookie, would become the starting center in a surprise move. It all started when Ringo brought an agent to Vince Lombardi to negotiate a better contract and more money. Lombardi didn't deal with agents back then, and he was so incensed about it that he traded the center to Philadelphia in about ten minutes.

Bowman consequently became the starter and kept that position for the next ten seasons. But the last five years he played in constant, tremendous pain. He had incurred dislocations of both shoulders early in his career and they would bother him the rest of his playing time with the Packers.

Teammate Jerry Kramer, who played next to Bowman at the guard position, would write in his book, *Distant Replay*, "Bowman played with tremendous courage. His left shoulder kept popping painfully out of joint. Once he had it wired, but he delivered one crisp block, and the wires broke, and the shoulder flopped onto his chest. It looked grotesque. Even with my medical history, I didn't like looking at Bowman's shoulder. For his last seven seasons, he wore a leather harness that usually held the shoulder in place."

Domenic Gentile, the Packers' trainer during Bowman's career, wrote in his book, *Players I Have Known*, "Every Monday during the season, Ken came into the training room for therapy. Many times, he could not lift his arms above his chest. He would soak in the whirlpool for a while, just to try to loosen them up. Then we would slowly and painstakingly began to work on increasing his range of motion."

Not only did Bowman play with pain, but he also became one of the best centers in the NFL during his career. "He was great," said Bill Curry, who took over the starting center spot in 1966 when Bowman was too injured to play.

The next season, Bowman would become part of Packer lore when he and Jerry Kramer would team up for the block that cleared the way for Bart Starr to score the winning touchdown in a payoff game against the Dallas Cowboys in the famous 'Ice Bowl' game. The picture showing Starr scoring, has been published over and over through the years. However, Kramer got the publicity for making the key block.

Kramer would write later in his book, *Instant Replay*, "Bowman and I teamed up on the block that moved out Jethro Pugh and sprang Bart Starr for the winning touchdown. I must admit, I didn't give the Bow too much credit in my diary of the 1967 season. Kenny Bowman came up to me smiling and said, 'Don't take all the credit, Kramer. Don't take all the credit. I helped you with that block.' 'Shut up Bow, ' I said. 'You've got ten more years to play. You've got plenty of time for glory. I ain't telling anybody anything. If they think I made that block alone, I'm gonna let them think it.'"

Lombardi kept preaching that his players must learn to play while hurt. He was more than pleased when one of his players would display the kind of courage he admired. Trainer Domenic Gentile would write, "Kenny was the kind of guy who could play in pain, which Lombardi, of course, admired. Once, just a couple of days after one of his dislocations, he came into the locker room and demanded to be taped. Then he went out and hit the seven-man sled, as if nothing had happened. It was unbelievable. I think even Lombardi was surprised."

But Bowman didn't escape all of Lombardi's wrath. During the off-season, Bowman studied for his law degree, and when he made a mistake at practice, Vince often insulted him: "You're too stupid to play this game, let alone become a lawyer!"

The degrading criticism was "…belittling and unnecessary," said Bowman in the *Milwaukee Journal*, in June of 1971. "In many ways, he was much too harsh…with the players. As a man, I didn't like him, but as a coach, he [was] the greatest."

Tom Murphy, director and archivist for the Packer Hall

of Fame, who got to know Bowman after his retirement, told me, "Ken was considered a radical during the early 1970's when he took an active role on behalf of the Players' Union during their labor disputes with management. He both acted and looked the part, too. Just look at some of his football cards from the era."

After his retirement from football in 1973, he earned a law degree and spent 20 years in private practice in De Pere and Green Bay. Then, seeking a warmer climate, he and his wife moved to Tucson, Arizona, where he took a position in the Public Defender's Office. Recently retired, he lives in the Tucson area. Bowman was recognized for his courageous play when he was inducted into the Packers' prestigious Hall of Fame in 1981.

If Bowman was a long-shot to become the Packers' starting center for ten years, Larry McCarren was an even bigger surprise. McCarren was drafted as a very low, twelfth-round draft choice from the University of Illinois in 1973.

While McCarren spent the 1973 season on the Packer taxi squad, through hard work, he took the starting center position after Bowman retired the next season and held it for the next eleven years. McCarren is another example of an interior lineman playing through injury with little fanfare.

But his teammates recognized his unusual courage to play and perform at all-pro level when hurt. They called him 'The Rock' for his steady, tough, high-level performance while playing through injury.

Lynn Dickey, who was the Packers' quarterback for most of McCarren's career, told us, "He's the toughest player I've ever been around."

Bart Starr, McCarren's coach for ten years, gave him a fine tribute when he called McCarren a "...player's player and a leader."

McCarren played 162 consecutive games, the most of any center in Packer history. During that time, he played with a broken hand, broken fingers, and a large assortment of sprains, bruises, cramps and traumas.

PROFILES OF COURAGE • KEN BOWMAN & LARRY McCARREN

Ken Bowman, a starting center for the Packers for ten seasons – most of them with dislocated shoulders.
Packer Hall of Fame photo

McCarren has been broadcasting the Packers games since 1995. He is also a favorite of TV viewers in northeast Wisconsin as Sports Director at WFRV-TV.

Larry McCarren (nicknamee 'Rock') played 162 consecutive games at center even though he had numerous injuries.
Packer Hall of Fame photo

In 1980, he had a hernia operation during training camp. Three weeks later, still weak, he started in the Packers' opening game, keeping his consecutive game streak alive. After the first play, coach Starr sent a replacement onto the field; McCarren waved him off and continued to play the rest of the game.

His streak finally came to an end in 1984, when he suffered a painful pinched nerve in his neck and could not go on. He would miss the last three games of that season. When he tried to come back in 1985, McCarren realized it was time to retire.

McCarren was named to the NFL Pro-Bowl in 1982 and 1983. He would be the lowest-drafted Packer – 12th round, number 308 overall – to go to the Pro-Bowl. He was also named to NFL All-Pro status in 1982.

After retirement from the Packers, McCarren joined WFRV-TV in Green Bay where he became sports director. He is probably better known for his role as part of the Packers' radio broadcast team. He first joined the team's broadcast in 1995, working his first four seasons with Jim Irwin and Max McGee, and now, with Wayne Larrivee.

McCarren and Larrivee provide broadcasts together across the Packer Radio Network. Though both are veteran broadcasters, the two were paired for the first time in 1999 to bring the color and excitement of Green Bay Packers football to fans throughout Wisconsin, Upper Michigan and four more-distant states.

McCarren has been voted Wisconsin 'Sportscaster of the Year' by the National Sportscaster and Sportswriters Association three times – 1994, 1996 and 2002. The iron-man center was recognized for his tenure with the Packers by being inducted into the Packers Hall of Fame in 1992.

Bowman and McCarren are two imposing examples of those offensive interior linemen who courageously play on through injuries and other obstacles.

The 'Ice Bowl'

Packers' 1967 championship game against Cowboys, in bitter cold, test of wills and display of courage

The phone rang in Frank Gifford's hotel room in Green Bay at 6:30 in the morning. It was his wake-up call. "Good morning, Mr. Gifford. It's 6:30 am and the temperature is 20 degrees below zero."

As he climbed out of bed, Gifford shook his head in disbelief. "It can't be 20 below zero. There must be some mistake," he thought. But there was no mistake about how bitter cold it was in Green Bay that Sunday on New Year's Eve in 1967.

A cold front had moved in and the temperature early that morning was between 15 and 20 degrees below zero, with winds gusting nearly 30 miles an hour. By noon, the windchill factor fell to an unbelievable minus forty-six degrees. South of Green Bay, Milwaukee would record the lowest December temperature reading since 1924.

Gifford, the former New York Giant star, was in Green Bay as the one of three CBS television announcers covering the 1967 NFL championship game between the Packers and the Dallas Cowboys. The Packers have played in many memorable games, championships, and Super Bowls, but none can compare to the game now referred to as the 'Ice Bowl.'

What sets this game apart from all the others was the cruel arctic weather that came blasting in that day, transforming the game into a fight for human survival. With a strong wind and temperatures dropping to 20 degrees below zero before the end of the game, on a rock-hard, frozen Lambeau Field, the Packers and Cowboys courageously managed to endure the intolerable weather conditions. The game required an unparalleled display of human values, courage and incredible resolve by two teams that pushed themselves to the limit.

It's no wonder that the 'Ice Bowl' is considered the greatest game ever played. You could also say it was the greatest display of team courage on a football field.

There had never been a game like it. It provided a test to determine players' intestinal fortitude, focus, mental toughness, self-discipline, and whether they had an insatiable desire to excel. It called into play Vince Lombardi's credo that he had been instilling into his players since the day he arrived as head coach and general manager nine years earlier.

The game would provide a stage for the Green Bay players to demonstrate to the entire sports world for one last time, how Lombardi's leadership had been so totally ingrained into their minds, hearts, and wills. It was to be the last time Lombardi would stand on the sidelines at Lambeau and coach the Packers.

To make the task more difficult, age and injuries were catching up with the Packers. Jimmy Taylor and Paul Hornung were gone. Their replacements, Jim Grabowski and Elijah Pitts had been injured earlier in the season. Nevertheless, Lombardi desperately wanted to prove he could go to the second Super Bowl without them.

Besides, Lombardi and Tom Landry had coached together with the Giants before becoming head coaches elsewhere, and had played several memorable games against each other, the most notable being the Packers' narrow victory against the Cowboys the year before in the NFL championships.

The Cowboys, on the other hand, were a better team than their 1966 club. They fully expected to beat the Packers in this game.

However, the bizarre, frigid conditions got into the Cowboys players' heads and began to create some doubt. Certainly not used to anything resembling this kind of cold weather, the players began to doubt how they would ever be able to perform in these terrible conditions.

As the players came out onto the field before the game for warm-ups, most had their hands tucked inside their plants as they slipped and skidded on the frozen turf. Every breath they took iced their nostrils and felt like an arrow shooting into their lungs.

Unfortunately, Lombardi's underground heating system for the field at Lambeau had failed. The field was nearly rock hard by game time. Toward the end of the game, the field had also formed razor-sharp edges on its concrete-like surface. Players' arms, hands, and knees were cut open.

Ray Scott, Jack Buck and Frank Gifford sat huddled in the CBS television booth, trying to stay warm but failing. Gifford's 'hot' coffee became frozen solid within minutes. All three had trouble announcing words before the end of the game.

The refs had to get a sporting goods store to open on Sunday so they could get warm clothing. Most of the 50,000 attending fans had come to Lambeau Field dressed in gear suitable for prolonged ice fishing. They came trudging into the stadium, huddled in insulated snowmobile suits, sleeping bags and wearing several layers of longjohns and flannel, along with heavy boots, warm hats and face masks. Those dressed in anything less were gone by the end of the first quarter.

Makeshift dugouts were set up for the players along the sidelines. Propane tanks were set up to heat the dugouts and the players, but they turned out to be almost useless against the bone-cold conditions.

As the teams lined up for the opening kick-off, the estimated windchill was minus forty-six degrees. It was, by far, the coldest game in NFL history.

As one of the refs tried to blow his whistle to start the game, there was only a brief, low-sounding 'tweet.' The whistle was frozen. As the ref pulled the whistle from his mouth, he tore his lip that was stuck to the ice-cold whistle. Blood dripped from the tear and immediately froze into a red icicle. The refs just yelled out the rest of the game. Whistles were useless.

As the game opened, players ran as though they were tiptoeing on eggs. As they tried to get traction, they slipped, skidded and bounced against the frozen field. Second-year halfback, Donny Anderson, and journeyman newcomer, Chuck Mercein, were both in the starting backfield with Bart Starr.

Mercein had joined the Packers in mid-season, after injuries had taken out the starters. He played seldom in his back-up role. Mercein, having been cut from the Giants, had been playing on a semi-pro team in 1967, when Lombardi called him to ask if he would join the Packers. Shocked and surprised beyond words, Mercein told Lombardi he would be on the next plane to Green Bay.

Little did he or Lombardi then realize what a critical role he would play on that Sunday.

The Packers moved the ball early against the Cowboys. They moved 82 yards, eating up nine minutes in sixteen plays and finishing the drive-off with a Starr-to-Boyd Dowler pass of eight yards for a touchdown. The Packers led, 7-0. In the second quarter, Lombardi used Ben Wilson and rookie Travis 'Roadrunner' Williams in the backfield, and the Packers continued to dominate.

The Cowboys' offense, led by Don Meredith, Don Perkins, Dan Reeves and Lance Rentzel was sluggish in the bitter cold. The Packers scored again in the second quarter, on a deep pass of 43 yards from Starr to Dowler. Packers led, 14-0.

As the Cowboys' defense began to dig in and get more assertive, the Packers became more conservative in the play calling. With five minutes left in the first half, Starr was

Profiles of Courage • ICE BOWL

Packer fans came dressed in snowmobile suits, sleeping bags, blankets, and face masks for the Ice Bowl game with Dallas, Dec. 31, 1967. One fan died of a heart attack, while many were treated for frostbite in the bone-chilling, minus 46 degrees.

Green Bay's Vince Lombardi has something to smile about on the sidelines during the 1967 NFL Championship.

UPI/Bettman News photo

hammered. He fell and fumbled going down. The Cowboys' big George Andrie picked up the loose ball and ran in for the touchdown. Packers 14, Cowboys 7.

With 1:50 left, Willie Wood fumbled a Dallas punt on the Green Bay 15-yard line and the Cowboys recovered it. The Cowboys were stopped as linebacker Ray Nitschke and Lee Roy Caffey made bone-crunching tackles all over the field. Villanueva kicked a field goal as time ran out in the first half. Packers 14, Cowboys 10. The Cowboys had not gotten a first down in the second quarter, but had put ten points on the board with the help of the two fumbles.

The halftime program was cancelled while the frozen fans tried to survive. Sitting there, no matter how well dressed, was sheer torture. One man died of a heart attack during the game. Several others passed out due to the severe cold. Others were treated for frostbite. As the day wore on, the breath from the fans created a kind of unified fog – a frozen vapor causing an eerie-looking haze over the stands.

Lombardi gave his players a tongue lashing in the locker room at halftime and the Packers came out more determined in the second half. However, the Cowboy defense seemed to be gaining in confidence and the Packers could not get their offense in gear as the playing surface continued to deteriorate. The score remained 14-10, Packers, as the fourth quarter began. On the first play, the Cowboys pulled a surprise that caught the Packers off guard.

Halfback Dan Reeves took a pitchout from Meredith, ran wide, as if to run – stopped suddenly, slid briefly on the frozen field, gained his footing and then threw to a wide-open Lance Rentzel for a touchdown. Cowboys 17, Packers 14.

As the fourth quarter wore on, both teams were moving slower. With their bodies now stiff, frozen to the bone and beaten up from the hard play and concrete-like field, every move was pure torture. Cowboy players said Meredith's face and lips were so numb, they couldn't understand him when he tried calling out plays in the huddle.

With less than five minutes left, the Packers took over on their own 32. As Nitschke and the rest of the Packer defense came off the field, he shouted twice in a gruff, hoarse voice to Starr and the offense, "Don't let me down."

With time running out, Starr called the first play in the huddle. They all knew this would probably be their last chance to score. Starr would later say, "When I looked at the faces of my team in the huddle, I saw a determination in their eyes. I knew we would score!"

Starr started the drive with a short pass to Anderson, and then Mercein ran for a first down. Starr to Dowler at the Dallas 42, then Starr to Anderson for 12 more. Two minutes left.

Starr to Anderson for nine yards to the Cowboys 30.

As the sun began to set in the late afternoon, the wind and cold increased. It was now an unbelievable 69 below zero with the windchill factor.

Mercein mentioned to Starr in the huddle that he could get open on the left flat. Starr faked a handoff to Anderson, turned to his left and threw a short pass to a wide-open Mercein, who rambled 20 yards to the Dallas 11 before stumbling out of bounds – 1:11 left.

Starr called Mercein's play again on a quick opener. The line opened a huge hole in the Dallas front four. Mercein ran all the way to the three-yard line before he was stopped. 54 seconds left.

Anderson was stopped for no gain on two successive running plays. Starr called time out with 16 seconds remaining. He told Lombardi at the sidelines, "Let's call '1931 wedge,' but instead of handing it off, I'll keep it and carry it in myself."

Lombardi said, "Run it and let's get the hell out of here."

Starr returned to the huddle and called '31 wedge.' None of the players knew Starr intended to keep the ball instead of handing it off to Mercein.

Looking at the ground for better footing, the Cowboy front four of Lilly, Pugh, Towns and Andrie anxiously kicked and scraped at the unyielding, frozen turf. They firmly prepared for one last determined stop.

When the ball was snapped, Starr kept the ball and pushed toward the goal line. A surprised Mercein, quickly making sure he was not called for a penalty, held his arms up high, showing the refs he had not pushed Starr as he fell over him.

Meanwhile, center Ken Bowman and guard Jerry Kramer completed the most photographed block in NFL history as Starr slipped over the two of them for the winning touchdown and the 21-17 win. It was the Packers' third straight NFL championship.

So, with just under five minutes to play and trailing 17-14, the Packers went 68 yards in 12 plays and scored with 13 seconds left. It was one of the greatest drives of all time.

Lombardi, Starr and others would weep openly in the locker room after the game. Total exhaustion and cold-numbed limbs left players from both teams in states of mild shock. The Cowboy locker room was total gloom.

Many fans stormed Lambeau Field and tore down the goal posts. Meanwhile, in their locker room, the Packers' form of subdued celebration was one of mild, exhausted contentment, knowing they had performed an almost unbelievable feat that afternoon – one that would be written and talked about for generations to come.

PROFILES OF COURAGE • ICE BOWL

The 'signature' play that put Lambeau Field into the national spotlight. The Packers defeated the Cowboys in bitter cold in a test of wills and display of courage.
Packer Hall of Fame photo

Lynn Dickey

*An amazing display of grit
in overcoming crippling injuries*

Football is physically demanding at any level – from high school through college. To play in the NFL – take it up several notches. The players are bigger, faster, and stronger.

Action at the pro level can be turbulent and violent. Too often, it becomes bone-crunchingly rough. Bodies take a constant beating. Many a gifted athlete has experienced a promising career in the pros get cut short with a crippling injury.

Lynn Dickey, a former Packer star in the 1970's and 1980's, could have, and in all reality, should have been just such a player. An outstanding high school athlete, who excelled in several sports and who was an All-Big-Eight quarterback at Kansas State, Dickey sustained not one, but several, severe injuries early in his NFL career. Any one of the three should have ended his ambition to play football in the NFL.

But they didn't. In an unbelievable display of unusual courage and with passionate persistence, Dickey overcame the crippling injuries that cost him two full seasons and parts of three others to become one of the Packers' all-time best quarterbacks, behind only two legends, Brett Favre and Bart Starr.

Dickey's early football career was the stuff of legends.

He quarterbacked the Osawatomie (Kansas) High team to an undefeated state championship in 1966. At Kansas State University, Dickey's name was honored for all time in 1996 when AP named him the greatest quarterback in the history of the Big Eight conference. It was at K-State that Dickey passed for 6,208 yards and 29 TDs. He passed for more than 380 yards four times with a high of 439 yards against Colorado in 1969. A two-time All-Big-Eight quarterback, Dickey was drafted by the Houston Oilers in 1971.

After breaking numerous passing records at Kansas State, the 6'-3", 214-pound Dickey was drafted by the Oilers, where he backed up Dan Pastorini. It was in the first quarter of the first exhibition game of 1972, against the St. Louis Cardinals, that the promising second-year quarterback received a crushing injury that would have ended football for most men.

"I was back to pass," Dickey recalls, "and I had to take off running. But this guy jumped on my back. He never really hit me, but I was carrying him piggyback for a few steps before I collapsed. I couldn't get my hands down and I hit hard on my knee, and the pressure kind of forked my hip out."

The next day, Dickey was operated on in Boston. His hip had been dislocated and the socket fractured. After the operation, he spent the next three weeks flat on his back and not moving. But contrary to some stories that say the doctor felt he may never walk again, his doctor actually never feared for Dickey's football career, though he did wonder about his patient's decision to continue to play football.

"The doctor told me I could play football again, but it would be up to me how much work I wanted to do building myself back up," Dickey recalled.

Following the operation, he sustained nerve damage in his leg while in traction for the better part of three weeks. He lost his reflex in his left Achilles tendon and had what is called a 'drop foot.' The pain was so excruciating that he received three sets of six shots in his spinal column, daily, before it finally started to subside.

After those first three weeks of lying flat on his back in traction, it took a few more days just to get out of bed because of dizziness, and then it was three more weeks of learning how to get up and down the hallway on crutches.

Finally, Dickey returned to Houston, only to have a painful nerve problem develop in his foot as a result of the original injury and surgery. So it was into a Houston hospital for three more painful weeks.

But as he suffered through the painful after-effects of his hip surgery and nerve pain, Dickey wondered, fleetingly, what might happen if he quit football. Still, he told me, "I never felt like giving up. I figured it was going to take time to recover, but I would never give up."

It was in the second week of November, almost four months after he suffered his hip injury, Dickey recalls, "I woke up one morning and the pain in my foot from the nerve was gone. Just like that."

But, on Christmas, he was still walking with a cane. Early in January, following the 1972 season, however, he was able to begin working out, though he had lost 40 pounds from his normal playing weight and was a shell of his former self.

"When I first tried to jog, I couldn't make it around the football field, even once," he said. But he kept running, day after day. Then he began lifting weights to build himself back up. Dickey recalled, "I didn't lose sight of my goals and wouldn't let any negative thoughts in." And by the time the Oilers opened camp in July of 1973, he was ready to report, though still weak and not in very good shape.

"It wasn't until the season was over that I really felt the strength coming back, "Dickey said.

Nevertheless, during that 1973 season, Dickey started four games for Houston with no ill effects. In fact, he engineered the Oilers' only win that season.

After two more seasons in Houston, playing backup to Pastorini, Dickey came to the Packers in a trade that coach and general manager Bart Starr engineered. Starr sent quarterback John Hadl, cornerback Ken Ellis and two draft

PROFILES OF COURAGE • LYNN DICKEY

Left: Dickey had to back up David Whitehurst in 1979 while he played himself back into shape.

Right: Dickey came back from three serious injuries that should have ended his career, but in an unusual display of courage, he returned to the field each time.
Packer Hall of Fame photo

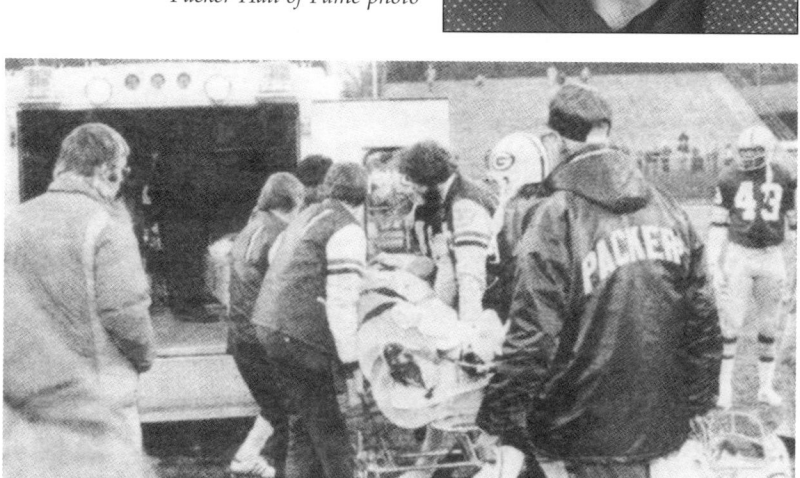

Dickey suffered a broken leg on the final play of a game in 1977. Dickey was booed in the 24-6 loss.

PROFILES OF COURAGE • LYNN DICKEY

Left: Lynn Dickey threw for 387 yards against the Redskins – and three touchdowns in the highest scoring "ABC Monday Night" game.

Right: Familiar sight: Another touchdown, and Dickey (12) gets congratulations from running back Eddie Lee Ivery.

Quarterback Lynn Dickey, in action vs. Rams, was voted Packers' MVP on offense in 1984 for the second year in a row.

choices to the Oilers for Dickey.

Known for his poise and canon-like arm, Dickey became the Packers' starting quarterback in 1976, but went out with a painful and serious shoulder separation against the Bears in mid-November. He again had surgery and could not return for the remaining four games.

Back at starting quarterback in 1977, Dickey had to run an offense with little receiver talent and a mediocre running game. It was one of the worst Packer teams of the 1970's. Dickey took a pounding that season, as the talent-thin Packers stumbled to a 2-6 record by mid-season. They played the 6-2 Los Angeles Rams in Milwaukee, where Dickey would receive yet another crushing injury. Once again, it should have ended his career.

The Milwaukee fans, in a foul mood from watching the Packers' poor play, were booing Dickey that Sunday, even though the Rams had roughed him up all day. The Packers picked up a touchdown in the third quarter on a 65-yard Dickey pass to Steve Odom, but to add fuel to the fired-up fans, Chester Marcol missed the extra point in the Rams' 24-6 win.

On the Packers' final play of the game, Dickey completed a 12-yard pass to Willard Harrell. Dickey was hammered to the ground after releasing the pass. He suffered a broken leg, was carried off the field on a stretcher and didn't play again until two years later, in 1979.

Art Daley, sports editor for the Green Bay *Press-Gazette* recalled the game. "There were mixed feelings among the fans after the game. Like one spectator said, 'Here we were booing him [Dickey] like crazy and then he breaks a leg. You don't feel right booing.' Early in the game, somebody in the press box said, 'If they don't keep the pressure off Dickey, he won't finish the game.' After the game, Coach Bart Starr was quite broken up and his voice was choked with emotion as he addressed the media, referring to the booing and Dickey."

The break in Dickey's left leg was worse than first expected. It was broken in not one, but two places. They

PROFILES OF COURAGE • LYNN DICKEY

An amazing display of grit in overcoming crippling injuries

Lynn Dickey closed out a 10-year Packer career and became the No. 3 passer in Packer history behind Bart Starr and Brett Favre.

took Dickey from the stadium to Milwaukee County Hospital, where an intern set the leg. However, the Packer physician was not happy with the set and performed extensive surgery in Green Bay the next day.

In Green Bay, Dickey was in a leg cast for four months before beginning daily workouts that included running one mile. When he complained that he still had a lot of pain, they took him to Mayo Clinic. It was there he found out his leg was still broken and not healing.

Unbelievably, he had been running and working out on a broken leg. More surgery was performed, including a long metal rod being driven down from his kneecap through the lower leg. Dickey was once again on crutches, for another six weeks, before he went to his kid's high school swimming pool and began swimming one mile every day.

Slowly and painfully, Dickey pushed and punished himself back into playing shape, but it took the entire 1978 season. In the meantime, with David Whitehurst at quarterback, and rookie receiver James Lofton, complementing a solid running attack led by Terdell Middleton and Barty Smith, the Packers improved to 8-7-1.

When Dickey, still trying to play himself back into game shape, returned to the Packers in 1979, Whitehurst was still the starting quarterback for most of the season. However, the promise of improvement the Packers showed in 1978 was gone. Dickey regained his starting position late in the season, but the Packers finished a disappointing 5-11.

It's hard to conceive that Dickey's most productive years as a quarterback came nearly 10 years after he was drafted out of college and *after* all those crippling injuries. It was poetic justice that overcoming three nearly career ending injuries, Dickey, in his mid-30's, had five outstanding seasons, from 1980 through 1984, before he tailed off in 1985 and finally retired. In 1983, he led the league with 4,458 passing yards, 32 touchdowns, and 9.2 yards per attempt.

In an unforgettable 1983 Monday Night Football duel with the Washington Redskins at Lambeau Field, Dickey led the Packers to a 48-47 win. He completed 22 of 30 passes for 387 yards and three touchdowns.

On October 12, 1980, Dickey completed 35 of 51 passes for 418 yards, including 15 straight completions versus Tampa Bay.

In the 1982 home opener at Milwaukee County Stadium, trailing the L.A. Rams, 23-0, at halftime, Dickey threw three touchdowns passes and led a furious 35-point comeback in the second half to help the Packers win, 35-23.

In the 1982 playoff battle with the St. Louis Cardinals, Dickey bombed the Cards with 260 yards passing, including touchdown tosses to James Lofton of 60 and 20 yards, and a seven-yarder to John Jefferson.

During those most productive years with the Packers in the 1980's, Dickey also had a much better group of receivers – James Lofton, John Jefferson and Paul Coffman. In addition, with Eddie Lee Ivory and Gerry Ellis, the running game was better, which opened up the passing for Dickey. While his major injuries were behind him, he still had numerous lesser injuries. He broke his thumb and two bones in his back, but never missed a game.

Dickey, still one of the most popular Packers, ranks third in the Packer record book in yards passing, touchdowns and highest passer rating (73.8). He can, and should, be considered one of the Packers' most productive quarterbacks – along with Brett Favre and Bart Starr.

But for raw-boned courage and perseverance to overcome extremely severe and potentially career-ending injuries – he perhaps should be considered in a class all by himself.

Looking back now, Dickey told me, "I loved playing the game…and even the practices. I didn't want to wake up one day when I was older and regret not giving it all I had to play as long as I could. I'm happy I didn't give up. I have no regrets."

LeRoy Butler

An inspiring story of overcoming disability and poverty

He was an All-Pro defensive back for the Packers in the mid-90's, but when he was a kid, he couldn't even walk. LeRoy Butler's success story as a football player is all the more inspiring, considering all the obstacles he had to overcome.

His African-American family was dirt poor and he wore leg braces as a youth. Yet, he overcame overwhelming odds to make it as a high school and college football All-American, and All-Pro as a Green Bay Packer favorite for eleven years.

From a disabled youth, spending much of his childhood in leg braces, LeRoy Butler went on to become the most durable defensive back in the history of the Green Bay Packers. Playing in 181 games, more than any other defensive back, the flamboyant Butler was a starter ever since his second season in 1991.

A recognized team leader, Butler was consistently productive. He is fourth-ranked interception leader in team history (38) and often sacked the opposing quarterback from his safety position.

But reaching star status as a football player was the furthest thing in mind for the Butler family in Jacksonville,

Florida, back in the early 1970's. Raised by his mother, who maintained a strong religious faith in spite of their poverty, LeRoy and his brothers and sisters grew up in one of the poorest neighborhoods of Jacksonville. They lived in a small, dingy apartment in the 'projects' that was bitterly cold and damp in the winter while being hot and oppressively muggy in the summer.

The doctors determined about a year after his birth, in 1968, that LeRoy had clubfeet and would need corrective surgery. The medical procedure included breaking his feet to reposition them.

He was then put into a body cast that ran from his chest to his feet. When the cast came off many months later, little LeRoy was fitted with heavy leg braces to keep his feet straight and separated from each other.

As he grew over the next few years, he continued to wear the leg braces that ran from his knees down to his shoes. They told his mother the braces would eventually straighten his feet and ease his constant pain, but the doctors warned LeRoy's mother it would take years before he could walk without the aid of his braces.

Just walking or going up stairs was painful and difficult for LeRoy as he reached school age. Getting dressed was also a daily challenge. Every day, LeRoy would lie on his bed while his mother and sister helped pull up his pants over his braces.

By the time he entered second grade, his classmates were playing basketball and baseball in the neighborhood playgrounds, but LeRoy could only sit on his porch and watch and dream of the day he might join them.

It was around this time in his life, as a six-year-old, that LeRoy began to form a strong faith. He said it really began when an orthopedic specialist told LeRoy that one day he would walk without the braces – not now, but someday.

Armed with that encouragement, Butler would say later, that was about the time he began his daily conversations with God. He attended church so often, the adults started calling him 'Little Deacon.' In his 'talks' with God, LeRoy

PROFILES OF COURAGE • LEROY BUTLER

LeRoy Butler was an All-Pro defensive back for the Packers in the mid-90's, but when he was a kid, he couldn't even walk.

Packer Hall of Fame photo

kept asking for the day he might be able to walk and run again like the other kids.

The doctors thought if they put his legs into the casts again, it might speed up the process. So once again, LeRoy's legs were put into casts from the knees down. He wore the them to class for several months, trudging back and forth to school.

At the end of the period, the casts came off and the doctors concluded more surgery would be unnecessary. However, LeRoy would have to continue leg braces, so back on went the heavy, 15-pound metal braces.

The doctors also gave him a wheelchair to help him get around when he got tired of clomping around with the braces. He hated the wheelchair and seldom used it.

Around this time, he began to make a game out of going up and down their stairs. As hard as it was with those 15-pound leg braces, LeRoy went up and down the steps, trying to improve the time it took each time.

One day, when he was eight, a 'miracle' took place, at least that's how LeRoy and his family saw it. One evening, LeRoy got angry at his sister, Vicki, for accidentally knocking him over and out of his wheelchair, breaking one of the braces. He jumped up and started stomping his feet, causing the other leg brace to break.

Butler recalled the incident in his autobiography, *The LeRoy Butler Story*. "'Look what you made me do!' I yelled at her. Vicki looked at me and started crying. That's when I realized both of my braces were broken. 'You're standing without your braces,' she screamed. I thought she was crying because I had yelled at her, but she was the first to realize something wonderful had happened. During my tantrum over the broken brace, my stomping broke the other one. At first, we all feared my legs would break from the pressure I was putting on them."

While LeRoy stood there in amazement, his mother came into the room and began to cry. Butler said in his book that it was a moment he would never forget. His brothers and sisters cried. His mother cried and repeated, over and over, "Thank you, Jesus! Thank you, Jesus!"

Other family members and neighbors began showing up to see LeRoy's 'miracle.' He was so excited, he couldn't sit still. When his mother gave him the OK to go outside, he went out into the night and began to run through the darkened streets. Later, he said he felt like Forrest Gump in his first run in the Tom Hanks movie.

Miracle or not, he now could walk and run. The braces were gone forever.

By the time he got into junior high school, LeRoy, after strenuous exercises, was strong enough to go out for football and basketball. He ran for a 62-yard touchdown in his team's second game that season.

In his junior year in high school, he made first team and ran for a 40-yard touchdown the first time he got the ball. He would earn a varsity letter that fall, but his family couldn't afford the letter jacket to put it on. His coach, Corky Rogers, came through for LeRoy and he got the jacket.

LeRoy played offense and defense his senior year. Now, at six feet and 185 pounds, he became a star player. He would be named to the Bally All-American team that year. He had gone from a cripple to a celebrity in a short time.

Then, one of LeRoy's fondest dreams, to play for the football powerhouse, Florida State, became a reality. When coach Bobby Bowden visited him at their humble apartment and offered LeRoy a football Scholarship, he thought he was dreaming.

He was a substitute his sophomore year, became a first-string safety as a junior, was cornerback his senior year, and went on to All-American honors. In Butler's book, Bobby Bowden said, "LeRoy Butler was not only an All-American football player, but also an outstanding person. His character stands out like a bright star. I never enjoyed coaching a player more than I did LeRoy. Happy personality, honest and conscientious. He has it all! I can call him my 'Brother.'"

The Packers drafted Butler in their second round, and while he was excited to play professional football, he wasn't even sure where Green Bay was located. When then Packer coach, Lindy Infante, congratulated him on the phone and asked if LeRoy had any questions, Butler answered, "Only one: Where's Green Bay?" (from *The LeRoy Butler Story*)

Butler became a starter in his second season and remained there until he retired after the 2001 season because of a disabling shoulder injury. Butler is given credit as the originator of the 'Lambeau Leap' for jumping into the end zone stands after he took a fumble in for a touchdown in 1993.

LeRoy Butler's spontaneous gesture after scoring a 1993 touchdown has turned into the team's most prominent modern tradition, and is emulated by many other players. Ironically, it also symbolizes the team's unique relationship with its fans. No doubt, the initial "Lambeau Leap" will go down as one of the most memorable moments of Butler's 12-year career.

Butler's leap took place in a frigid game versus the Los Angeles Raiders on December 26, 1993, at Lambeau Field. The touchdown gave the Packers a commanding fourth-quarter lead en route to a 28-0 shutout.

Selected to the Associated Press All-Pro team four years in a row in the mid-90's, Butler was also named to the NFL 1990's All Decade team and was inducted into the Packer Hall of Fame in 2007.

Butler's courageous story can be an inspiration to anyone fighting poverty and disability. Butler is still doing his part to help the disadvantaged. In Jacksonville, within a mile of where he grew up, he set up the LeRoy Butler Foundation to help kids in the inner city.

Ron Wolf, former Packer general manager, was quoted in The *LeRoy Butler Story* as saying, "LeRoy is tough, a leader, compassionate, tough, has a respect for the game, thorough, tough, understanding, consummate player at his position. I said he was tough, but as good as he was as a football player, he is even a better person!"

Donald Driver
Provides hope in overcoming financial hardships with lessons learned as a youth

Donald Driver, a low-round draft pick by the Packers in 1999, through hard work and an extreme physical fitness program, has become one of the NFL's top receivers. His strong desire to excel was instilled at an early age, when as a youth, he witnessed and lived through the hardships of watching his mother raise him and his four siblings by herself.

Divorced when Donald was only three, his mother, Faye, vowed to keep her family together and do whatever it took, even as a single mother. Few youngsters have had to go through the financial hardships his family endured while he was growing up in Houston in the 1970's and 1980's.

The middle child in a five-sibling family, Donald often saw his mother skip meals while holding down several jobs, including night work. During his youth, there were several holidays he would spend without his mother, and for a time, he had to live with his grandmother, while Faye worked to make ends meet.

There was a time in his early teens when his mother just couldn't keep up with the bills. A collection agency confiscated all their possessions, forcing them to live out of a U-Haul truck. At one point, Driver remembers, they slept several nights in motel rooms his mother paid for with food stamps. Gifted with a quick mind and even quicker body, Driver overcame these hardships to become a star athlete in high school, lettering four times each in track, football, basketball, and baseball at Milby High School in Houston. He was good enough to earn a full scholarship at Akron State in Mississippi. Without the scholarship, there would have been no way he would have been able to afford college.

Driver continued to excel in sports in college where he starred in track and football. But it was in football that he made his name, receiving conference honors and leading his team in receptions his senior year.

Driver didn't play much the first season the Packers drafted him in 1999, but since then, he has become the ultimate professional, and simply keeps getting better with age. He has become an irreplaceable weapon for quarterback Brett Favre, and one of the NFC's top wideouts year after year. After setting career highs in receptions and yards in 2004, and surpassing them in 2005, he bumped those personal marks up yet again in 2006, his eighth season, with 92 catches for 1,295 yards, to earn his second Pro Bowl appearance.

Those totals ranked second and third in the NFC, respectively. Both were fifth in the NFL in 2006, and his career-high, 191-yard performance at Minnesota on November 12, 2007, was the best single-game total by any NFC receiver on the season.

Driver wants to play for another seven years, and there's no doubting he may do that with the tremendous care he takes of his body.

With the ability to play both flanker and split end, Driver continues to establish himself as one of the team's all-time great receivers by climbing on various lists in team record books.

On December 16, 2007, during a 33-14 victory over the St. Louis Rams, Brett Favre broke Dan Marino's all-time record mark of 61,361 career passing yards. It was appropriate that the new record came on a seven-yard completion to

PROFILES OF COURAGE • DONALD DRIVER

Donald Driver displays unusual courage to inspire young people.
Packer Hall of Fame photo

Driver – Favre's main receiver the last seven years.

In the NFC championship game on January 20, 2008, against the New York Giants, Driver also had the longest play in the playoffs of the Packers' franchise history with a 90-yard touchdown catch from Favre. Driver's outstanding year in 2007 earned him another trip to the prestigious Pro Bowl game in Hawaii at the end of the season.

But in spite of his success in football, Driver has not ignored the tough lessons he learned as a youth. Overcoming countless obstacles growing up has inspired him to become one of the team's most involved players in giving back to the community. In 2000, he and his wife, Betina, created the Donald Driver Foundation, which offers assistance to homeless mothers and underprivileged children in Green Bay and Houston.

In addition, Driver has made more than 430 appearances since 1999, from schools to youth football fields, to churches, delivering motivational speeches or offering assistance.

In 2007, Driver received a JB award for community service. The award is named for CBS' NFL Today host James Brown and is given to a select group of players for their individual contributions to their communities. Driver was also named the Packers' 'Walter Payton NFL Man of the Year' in 2002, in recognition of his extensive work in the community, and was chosen by *The Sporting News* as one of the NFL's 'Good Guys' in its July 5, 2004, issue.

Through his young age of 33, Driver has had the unusual courage to inspire other young people with financial hardships. He gives them hope to dream, and shows with his own life, that if you work hard, you can make them come true.

Brett Favre
*An amazing career that displayed
a special kind of courage*

One would think that any player in the NFL who starts an incredible, record-setting 253 consecutive regular-season games is either very lucky or one tough, courageous son-of-a-gun. In Brett Favre's case, it's probably a little of the first and a huge abundance of the latter.

Yes, Favre has been fortunate to have never sustained a severe injury during his professional career, and to have started every game for the Packers in nearly 16 consecutive years requires a rare kind of competitiveness and resolve never before seen in the entire history of professional football.

While leading the Packers to more winning seasons than any other quarterback in the NFL and shattering all sorts of records along the way, Favre had more than his share of obstacles to overcome – both physical and emotional. We'll cover just a few that occurred during his amazing career that displayed a special kind of courage.

During Favre's junior year in college at Southern Mississippi, he sustained a serious injury off the field that could have nipped his football playing days in the bud before they really got started. On a warm summer evening in 1990, Favre was driving home from a relaxing, fun day with his brother and a friend near Biloxi, Mississippi, when headlights from an oncoming car blinded him just long enough for him to miss a curve in the road, hit loose gravel, leave the highway and slam into a tree. His brother, Scott who had been driving behind him, stopped, got out of his vehicle, broke the car window and pulled out an unconscious Brett.

The seat belt had caused enough internal injuries, that the doctors had to remove over two feet of his small intestine. The operation might have meant the end of the season for a lesser athlete, but by the second game of the Southern Mississippi season, Favre was back to lead his team to an upset win over favored Alabama. He went on to start every game, the rest of that season and during his senior year. Favre set several passing records where his legendary toughness would first become evident.

The Atlanta Falcons drafted Favre. Once there, he sat on the bench and got in the coach's doghouse for underperforming, being overweight and missing some team meetings. In February of 1992, the Packers' general manager, Ron Wolf, traded a first-round draft choice for this young, really unknown quarterback. It was a bold move that would impact the Packers' fortunes for many years.

It didn't take long for Favre to step into the spotlight. When the Packers' popular quarterback, Don 'The Majik Man' Majkowski, went limping off Lambeau Field to the sidelines in the first quarter of the third game of the 1992 season, he didn't know he would never return – ever – as the Packer starting quarterback.

As Majkowski was helped off the field, with torn ankle ligaments, a young, inexperienced, raw kid by the name of Brett Favre came sprinting onto Lambeau turf to quarterback the team.

Many had thought the new general manager, Ron Wolf, had been nuts when he traded a number-one draft pick for the unknown quarterback from Atlanta earlier that year.

Favre would make Wolf look like a genius. True to storybook form, the brash, gun-slinging Favre led the Packers

PROFILES OF COURAGE • BRETT FAVRE

Above: An intense Favre gets ready to unload as he sets his sights on his target upfield his first year as a Packer.
Packer Hall of Fame photo

Right: Head Coach Mike Holmgren imparts some football philosophy to his quarterback Brett Favre.

to a win over the visiting Cincinnati Bengals with a 35-yard pass for a touchdown in the last 13 seconds of the game.

Favre took off his helmet, held it high and raced off the field. He became the Packers' starting quarterback ever since. The consecutive-games-played streak was started on that warm, sunny fall day in 1992. "When all those around you have doubt, he doesn't have the doubt," Wolf said that day. "That's what he possesses."

The next week, while Majkowski was healing from his injury, Favre led the team to victory; then his inexperience showed, when the Packers lost four of their next five games. Just when it looked as though Majkowski was ready to return, Favre pulled off six wins in a row before the Packers lost their last game of the season to finish 9-7 and in second place in the Central Division.

In the middle of the 1992 season, Favre suffered a serious injury that could have put him out of action. In the first quarter, in a game against the Philadelphia Eagles at Milwaukee County Stadium, Reggie White hammered him hard, separating Favre's shoulder. Majkowski peeled off his warmup jacket and started to warm up on the sideline, anticipating Favre would have to come out.

Instead, Favre got a painkiller shot in the shoulder at halftime and stayed in the game to lead the Packers to a 27-24 upset win over the Eagles. White later said that Favre had been the main reason he had signed with the Packers six months later.

Favre would incur several injuries over the next few seasons. Most notable was an extremely painful deep thigh bruise in a game against Tampa Bay in 1993. Limping around, he threw the game-winning touchdown on the first play after the injury.

In November of 1995, he suffered a severe ankle sprain against the Vikings. He missed most of the second half, spent the next several days on crutches, and didn't practice the following week. On game day the following Sunday against the Bears, Favre still had the sore ankle taped and re-taped and it felt like a cast. Unable to move around, he

Favre played the game of his life. It was an unbelievable performance. For those of us who were privileged to see this game, we sat in absolute, total amazement. Favre ended up passing for nearly 400 yards, threw for four touchdowns, and his aroused teammates help crush the Raiders, 41-7.

In October of the following year, with his streak still intact, Favre and Deanna got more bad news. Her brother Casey had been killed in an all-terrain vehicle accident. Four days later, while they were still recovering from that blow, Deanna learned she had breast cancer.

Favre managed to weather the emotional roller coaster and the Packers finished first in the NFC North.

The next season, 2005, would be difficult for Favre for a variety of reasons. Deanna was being treated for her breast cancer and the Packers were suffering a losing season – Favre's first as a Packer in 13 seasons. The team went 4-12, and coach Sherman got fired at the end of the season.

A variety of Favre's injuries were taking longer to heal than expected, and the mental strain of the long seasons was becoming more demanding for Favre. For the first time in the off-season, he wasn't sure he wanted to play anymore. New, young coach, bad team, "Do I really want to come back?" he asked himself. Besides, he loved his 465-acre home in Hattiesburg. He waited until April of 2006 to finally decide to come back.

While he did return, Favre did not have his usual outstanding season everyone had become so accustomed to.
It looked like he was fading. At age 37, he had lost his youthful appearance. His hair and five-day growth of whiskers were turning gray fast. His face showed deep lines around the eyes and mouth. Sad to say, Favre was beginning to look like an 'old man.'

The young Packers of 2006 did play better than expected and finished at 8-8. But Favre did not have a good year. At the end of the season, the new head coach, Mike McCarthy, told Favre bluntly that when he came back for the 2007 season, he simply had to play better for the team to improve.

PROFILES OF COURAGE • BRETT FAVRE

Right: The injuries kept building on Favre, to kill the pain, he turned to painkillers.
Milwaukee Journal photo

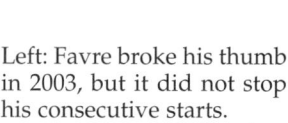

Left: Favre broke his thumb in 2003, but it did not stop his consecutive starts.
Sports Weekly photo

Brett Favre's family was one of many in the NFL affected by Hurricane Katrina.
AP Wire photo

least. He had a hard time getting up and had to have others help him after being sacked. When he was driven off the field to the locker room with a towel draped over his head, Packer fans feared the worst. He later said, "I thought I was done for the year."

He wasn't, but he did suffer a sprained lateral collateral ligament. If the Packers hadn't had the next week off, Favre's streak would have been broken. As it was, he wore his knee brace the rest of the season and went on to lead the Packers to a 12-4 season followed by the playoffs.

In October of the 2003 season, Favre broke the thumb on his right hand playing in St. Louis against the Rams. It wasn't enough to keep him out of action. With his thumb taped up, Favre kept playing the rest of the season. Again, a week off in the schedule helped this thumb heal and kept the streak alive.

Late in the 2003 season, the Packers were once again in first place and on the west coast, getting ready to play the Oakland Raiders. The day before the game, Favre got the news from Deanna that his Dad had died suddenly from a heart attack back in their home in Mississippi. Brett and Irv, who was only 58 years old, had been very close, so it came as a devastating shock. As Deanna wrote in her book, *Don't Bet Against Me,* she took their two daughters to a friend's house and she flew to Oakland, arriving at 3:00 A.M. She encouraged Brett to play in the game saying, "Your Dad was so proud of you, Brett. He came to every one of your college games and has watched all of your pro games – do you think he'd want you to sit out tomorrow? I'm convinced he would have wanted you to play." They fell asleep, holding onto each other.

When teammate Donald Driver visited Favre in his hotel room before the game, Favre told Driver he was going to play. "It is what Dad would want."

Driver said later, "Brett was hurting big time, but he said he was going to play because we were his family, too."

And play he did. Before a national television audience, choking back the tears and tremendous emotional strain, stood in the pocket, play after play, and carved the Bears up with his passing. He threw for 336 yards and five touchdowns, and the Packers won, 35-28.

The 11-5 1995 Packers got all the way to the NFC Championship game before losing to the Dallas Cowboys, 38-27. The Packers were rising and were ready to take the next step – the Super Bowl.

While the Packers were winning, Favre was performing at a tremendously high level. His QB rating for the 1995 season was a remarkable 99.5. He threw 38 touchdowns and only 13 interceptions. He was awarded the NFL MVP award that season. It would be the first of three – 1995, 1996 and 1997.

But he was also taking a beating, game after game, season after season. His body was now constantly in pain. So, he began to take painkillers, primarily Vicodin. "I was popping them like candy," he would later say. He had become addicted and he knew it. In the early summer of 1996, Favre checked himself into the Meninger Clinic in Topeka, Kansas, to begin rehab to get rid of the addiction.

It was 46 days later that he came out clean and cured, saying, "I began to see things more clearly. I had gotten sidetracked in some important ways." He also came out boasting, predicting the Packers would win the Super Bowl that season. Shortly after rehab, he and Deanna were married, and he also started the Brett Favre Forward Foundation that provides aid to disabled and disadvantaged kids in Wisconsin and Mississippi. A lot more happened to him in the rehab clinic than ridding himself of the addiction.

Favre's bold prediction came true – the Packers did go to the Super Bowl after the 1996 season, for the first time in 29 years. They did whip the Patriots, 35-21, while Favre completed 14 of 27 passes for 246 yards, threw two touchdown passes, and ran for another. The Packers went on to the Super Bowl again the next season, but lost to Denver.

Fast-forward to October 2002, and a game against the Washington Redskins at Lambeau. It was Brett's 164th-straight start, but came close to being his last, for a while at

During the off-season, Favre hired a personal trainer to work with him at his farm in Hattiesburg. Later, Favre turned up at the Packers' training camp in the best shape he had been in since the mid 1990's.

Finding out, after nearly three years of treatments for breast cancer, that Deanna was cancer-free also helped Brett to concentrate.

In the process of healing, Deanna emerged as an inspiration to others, displaying her own brand of courage. After her highly publicized battle with cancer, she wrote a book titled *Don't Bet Against Me – Beating the Odds Against Breast Cancer* and it immediately became a *New York Times* bestseller. As the founder of the Deanna Favre HOPE Foundation, she now travels the country to speak about the importance of early diagnosis, and raises funds to provide early diagnostic services, education and financial support for uninsured and underinsured women battling breast cancer. No doubt, Deanna provided her own kind of inspiration for Brett by the way she coped with her cancer and the loss of both her brother and stepfather, all within a couple of years.

Favre looked and played like he did back in the mid 1990's when he took the Packers to two Super Bowls. He overcame a separated shoulder and painful elbow injury to lead the youngest team in the NFL to a record of 13-3 and the NFC Championship playoff game against the New York Giants. They lost to the Giants, 23-30, in overtime, but they were only one game, and possibly one play, shy of the Super Bowl again.

After the game, Packer fans wondered if Favre would return for one more season and take this young team all the way. But now, the looming issue was not youth, but age, specifically, whether the 38-year-old quarterback would return for an 18th season. He decided not to come back.

Favre shattered numerous records in 2007. He broke Dan Marino's mark for career touchdown passes, and John Elway's mark for career victories by a quarterback. He even threw a 90-yard touchdown pass against the Giants, the longest in Packers play-off history.

Favre failed to engineer his 41st game-winning drive by the end of the fourth quarter, and not even in overtime, in the loss against the Giants. It would be Favre's last game, but afterward, he said the game did not influence his decision about retiring. "Had we won that game and gone on to the Super Bowl, whatever happened, I would go home and think about where I want to go from there," Favre said.

When he was named 'Sportsman of the Year' during the 2007 season by *Sports Illustrated*, reporter Alan Shipnuck wrote, "The Packers' 'iron man' is, at 38, enjoying one of his finest NFL seasons. His passing is more precise, his leadership more evident than ever, but his greatest attribute is the devotion he inspires in those he touches – and his dedication to making their lives better." When Shipnuck asked Favre for his favorite memory, Favre told him he would remember all the big victories, the touchdowns – but also the tough losses, and the times he was hurt and under emotional stress from issues off the field. He told the *Milwaukee Journal Sentinel*, "Those times when I've been down, when I've been kicked around, I hold on to those. In a way, those are the best times I've ever had, because that's when I've found out who I am, and what I want to be."

Favre's career as a Packer was truly amazing and remarkable in many ways. All those NFL passing records will take many years for someone else to break. Favre has said records don't define his great career, but I take issue with Favre about one of his records never being broken. His 250-plus consecutive regular season starts and over 20 post-season starts is his one proud record that truly *defines* his career *and* his character. In addition to having been blessed with a strong athletic body, Favre has also been also infused with a special kind of courage and joy for the game that he has displayed, again and again, these many years.

For young people looking for sports heroes to emulate today, let them focus on Brett Favre, not just for his accomplishments on the field, great as they were, but also for the boldness and courage it often took to either stay on the field, or take it, in the first place.

PROFILES OF COURAGE • BRETT FAVRE

Right: Brett Favre's father, Irv, was always around football, coaching a minor league team in 2001.
Photo courtesy South Mississippi Sun Herald

Left: In 2004, when his wife, Deanna, learned she had breast cancer, Favre took it hard, but she insisted he keep playing.
AP Wire photo

During his 16th season with the Packers, Favre performed as well as he had at any time in his career.
AP File photo

Favre has been on display long enough all these years for us all to watch him literally grow up and go through the trails of life – on and off the playing field. We may or may not remember some of those thrilling come-from-behind wins or those bullet-like passes that seemed impossible to complete – but no doubt we will surely remember the passion he brought to each game and the way he gallantly handled adversity while he was a Packer.

Postscript

Of the 18 men profiled in the preceding pages, eight are in the prestigious Pro Football Hall of Fame in Canton, Ohio. All except two have also been honored by inductions into the Packer Hall of Fame. It's just a matter of time before the remaining two, Donald Driver and Brett Favre, also get honored for their outstanding accomplishments as Packers.

While they all have been recognized for their successes on the field, I have tried to show an additional quality each posed – a rare kind of courage – both on and off the football field.

By no means was this project meant to include all former and present Packers displaying this courageous characteristic. Many more could and should have been chronicled in a book of this nature. There have been legions of men who have given evidence of their own kind of heroism throughout the nearly nine decades of the Packers' existence.

Nevertheless, I have focused on these few men, either because I was more familiar with them through previous research for other projects, or because I had interviewed them and gotten to know them personally.

The major point of their profiles is to show that, although these were gifted athletes or coaches who became some of the best in their profession, these men gave evidence to the fact they were not exempt from life's ups and downs.

There is a message here for all of us in learning how to overcome our own valleys. Their real-life stories give evidence to their character and thereby become models for each of us to follow in our own life experiences.

About the Author

David Zimmerman is also the author of four other books on the Green Bay Packers, including *In Search of a Hero – The Life and Times of Tony Canadeo* and *Lambeau, The Man Behind the Mystique*. He also co-authored two books with his son Stephen, on the History of the Green Bay Packers. He has written over 20 books on diverse subjects and is presently a member of the Board of Directors of the Green Bay Packers Hall of Fame. He and his wife, Peggy, and family live in Wisconsin.

For additional copies of
Legends of Lambeau – Packer Profiles of Courage,
and other books written by David Zimmerman,

visit the Web site of David Zimmerman at
www.david-zimmerman.com

or visit the Packer Hall of Fame Web site
www.packershalloffame.org

or mail a check for $24.95,
plus $5.00 for shipping and handling,
and payable to Eagle Books to:
Eagle Books
P.O. Box 253
Hales Corners, WI 53130